Collecting for Tomorrow

Collecting for Tomorrow

by
Brian Jewell

BLANDFORD PRESS

Poole   Dorset

First published in the U.K. in 1979
Copyright © 1979 Blandford Press Ltd
Link House, West Street
Poole, Dorset BH15 1LL

ISBN 0 7137 0937 5

British Library Cataloguing in Publication Data

Jewell, Brian, b.1925
    Collecting for tomorrow.
    1. Collectors and collecting
    I. Title
    790.13'2   AM231

*Set and printed in Monophoto Plantin 11/12pt by
BAS Printers Limited, Over Wallop, Hampshire and bound by Robert
Hartnoll Ltd.*

Contents

Preface

Unashamedly, this is a book concerned with collecting with a profit motive in mind. This may shock purists who often say, in all sincerity, that they collect with the sole desire of accumulating a complete series, or the most highly esteemed specimens, with no thought of selling. However, most members of this dedicated hard-core band of enthusiasts would hesitate before turning down a bargain that could result in a temptingly profitable deal.

So this book may be for the greedy. It is also intended for those who see nothing wrong with making some money out of an interest—which is what racecourse punters, allotment diggers, dog breeders, and stock exchange investors are doing all the time.

Acknowledgements

The author is grateful for the assistance of many people for providing illustrations and wishes especially to acknowledge the following:

Page 15, novelty egg cups, Sonia Roberts Features; page 31, baby carriages from the Baby Carriage Collection; page 47, domestic equipment, Frederick Wackett; page 48, domestic items, Archibald Kenrick and Sons Ltd; page 49, domestic items, Archibald Kenrick and Sons Ltd; page 56, ornamental design in cast iron, Archibald Kenrick and Sons Ltd; page 64, postcards, Valerie and Patrick Monahan; page 82, tobacco and snuff tins, Metal Box Co. Ltd; page 86, Pears soap advertisement, Graham Clark Publications; page 90, sweat shirt, Zoran Peshich for T. Shirt Monopoly; page 98, Marconiphone, The Marconi Co. Ltd; page 122 (lower), tin toy, Arno Weltens; Jacket, Mickey Mouse © Walt Disney Productions.

Introduction

To predict what will be collectable in the future is to invite criticism and to tread on many toes. A safe forecast could be that, like the products of all periods, those that are well designed and expressions of the age that produced them, will survive.

If we are to act on the basis of the first part of this statement, we have also to make a reasonably accurate appreciation of what will be considered 'good taste' or 'well designed' in times to come and, looking back over the past fifty years, such a forecast would seem very difficult, if not impossible. Who, for example, in the 1920s, 30s, or 40s, would have predicted that rectangular boxes, be they used as offices, residences, record players or furniture, would ever be considered the height of 'good taste'? This is the shape we call *functional*, though this claim is not strictly true; it may be easier to keep clean but cube-form does not exploit the full strength of the material from which it is made.

'An expression of the age that produced them' is, to this author, a primary qualification for a future collectable and it is this criteria that has been used throughout the book.

Profit aside, collecting should, first and foremost, be fun. There is something miserable about knowing that someone is stocking up with commemoratives or 'mint and boxed' die-cast model cars purely as an investment, or to have a visitor to your collection constantly ask 'how much is it worth?'. If we are honest, appreciation in value does matter but once this consideration becomes the main, or even sole, reason for collecting, it is not a great distance from the miser's candle and counting table.

Rarity, coupled with a trend in collecting, equates to high prices. Indeed, antique dealers trade on this very fact all the time. People are not craving to buy vintage television sets—not yet! In fact, the idea may seem ludicrous, but not so many years ago it was unthinkable that a cast iron and wooden mangle could have a fate other than being hit with a heavy hammer. That was until cast iron became fashionable, when 'real' materials became trendy in what has become a throw away world.

It is just that throw away philosophy and built-in obsolescence that causes objects around us—things we take for granted—to become rare, and some of them very rare indeed, within a few years of their manufacture.

Choose the product with thought and, given an element of luck in the fickleness of collecting trends, the rewards can be good. For example, a die-cast model traction engine, with a production run of hundreds of thousands, that retailed for 5 shillings and 6 pence ($27\frac{1}{2}$p) in the 1960s was, by the mid-1970s, commanding up to £10. One would have to be fortunate to realise that sort of return from more conventional investment. It is even possible to build up a profitable collection at no cost at all—printed tinplate boxes, bottles, postcards, matchboxes and beer mats—to mention but a few of the more commonly accepted divisions of 'junk' collecting.

Collecting for profit is like the rag trade. If a fashion can be anticipated, and if the individual has the strength of mind to stand by conviction and perhaps even to withstand ridicule, money will be made. Stevengraphs, fairings, Goss ware, and the like, had to wait many years before being accepted as collectors' items. Today's industrial products will not have this delay. Objects age quicker now, modifications are often made annually, and a higher percentage are consigned to the scrap heap.

Ideally, things collected should reflect social and economic conditions, as well as having that hard to define attribute that we call 'mood or flavour' of the moment—the lettering style and graphics in old advertisements illustrates this—it is, of course, why posters have achieved such popularity.

Appearance matters. Dealers always say they can charge more for something that will look right on a room divider, coffee table or shelf—not the mantelshelf; that useful parking space does not survive in latter day built houses. On the other hand it must be remembered that what looks ugly today could be considered the 'in thing' tomorrow—a smoothing iron or a sewing machine were thought of as anything other than ornamentation up to the recent past but now they are highly desirable, as any dealer worth his or her salt will relate.

Size must be considered—although this is not of paramount importance. There is little difficulty in off-loading last year's acquired traction engine or steamroller at a handsome profit. Nevertheless, small collectables are, understandably, quicker to gain popularity and value. They are also easier to transport and store.

Collecting for tomorrow requires elements of prophecy, patience and persistence, as well as some knowledge of manufacturing methods and trends. Good natured exchanges of information with dealers and fellow collectors, spiced with a little harmless collecting espionage, will go a long way towards success but, in the end, it must be admitted that collecting is an individualistic and even lonely craft—nay, art!

It is attempted in the following pages to suggest new collecting themes and to point out some of the currently more neglected subjects which will probably gain popularity in future. Many will raise a few eyebrows and possibly cause the odd disparaging exclamation, but picking the unexpected is what profit motivated collecting is about. It pays to remember that Goss ware, die-cast model cars, lead soldiers, sewing machines and typewriters were all dustbin fodder in the living memory of most of us.

Finally, it is essential, when the time comes to translate collected items into cash, to choose the buyer carefully. It is useless to eagerly rush along to a general antique dealer and expect a market price. A collector should establish, for himself, a register of dealers who specialize in the class of material. Trends at auction sales should be observed. Likewise, attempts should be made to contact and know where to find other collectors with similar interests. The value of anything is always what the buyer is prepared to pay, but there is someone, somewhere, who wants what we have for sale, and finding them is part of the game.

I   Collecting the Accepted

It is a case of choosing to be either a small fish in a large pool or a large fish in a small one. 'Accepted collectables' have been analysed, written about, dissected, praised, criticised, taken apart, and put together to an extent that would amaze their makers or originators, and to the bemusement of the newcomer.

Ceramics and glass, precious metal, furniture, antiquarian books, paintings, prints; anything to which the vague term *art* can be applied, has been so widely and well documented in recent years that one wonders what else can be contributed.

We get the feeling that it is difficult to go far wrong by sticking to the 'accepted collectables'. You 'pays yer money and takes yer choice' and the resulting collection will automatically appreciate in value. Why? Because the market is geared that way. The *art* subjects being the 'gold standard' of the trade in antiques and collectables.

This is all very well if a sufficient bank balance is available for the initial purchases and, secondly, if the collector is conventionally minded enough to follow the established lead. It is unlikely that such people will read this book, and certainly they will have received sufficient guidance from other and more expert sources to cause them to pass over lightly any advice that could be proffered by this author.

Therefore, it is not intended to dwell at length on the subjects with an already widely accepted appeal to collectors.

Prints and Limited Editions

It is hard to believe that limited edition prints, art reproductions and books will live up to the hope of the people who buy them, if they are thinking of substantial profit. These schemes seem to some collectors to be rather too conspired. If there is a limited edition of say, 1,000; because it is announced at the time of release and because each copy is numbered, it is unlikely that many will be scrapped or lost which means that the survival rate will be high—possibly well over 90 per cent. in the course of fifty years. A production run of perhaps 100,000 of say, a toy would, because it is a child's plaything, have a very low survival rate; and—once it becomes a collectable—it will be very rare and command many times its list price.

That, in a nutshell, is the philosophy behind this book.

Postage Stamps

It is not intended to dwell long on the collecting of postage stamps. The subject is so well known and more than enough has been written about stamps to make it unnecessary to try to win converts. Undoubtedly, postage stamps can be a good investment and there is plenty of guidance available for those attracted to this branch of collecting.

An interesting division of stamp collecting is that of the unofficial issues of British off-shore islands. Purists do not accept them and the philatelist's bible, *Stanley Gibbon's Catalogue*, does not list them. However, they do interest some collectors and they are slowly assuming respectability. At least, there is a book on the subject, *The Catalogue of British Local Stamps*, by Gerald Rosen. It lists stamps carrying the names of uninhabited and sparsely populated islands such as:

Brechou, off Sark
Caldey, off South Wales
Calf of Man
Canna, off Inverness-shire
Davaar, Mull of Kintyre
Eynhallow in the Orkneys
Gough in the Scillies
Herm in the Channel Islands
Heston, off Kirkcudbrightshire
Lihou in the Channel Islands
Long Island, County Cork
Lundy, Bristol Channel
Papay, Skye
Sanda, off Mull of Kintyre
Shuna, off Argyllshire
Soay, Skye

Straffa, off Mull
Stroma in Pentland Firth
Summer Isles, off Western Ross

These unofficial local stamps could well be worth collecting for tomorrow.

Egg Cups

Egg cups are becoming popular collectables and are well worth picking up in junk shops and jumble sales before prices soar, as they almost certainly will.

Egg cups have been made from the seventeenth century, and it has been mainly in Britain that the boiled egg became the accepted breakfast ingredient. In the great houses eggs were sent to the table by the dozen. As the kitchen could be a long way from the breakfast room, they arrived at the table uncooked, to be boiled in silver table-top burners heated by small spirit stoves.

Poorer families had Sheffield plate, electroplate, or pewter egg frames in which the eggs were brought to the table. These egg frames were simple circles of wire set round a central spindle. Some of the nineteenth century frames had recesses into which egg cups were slotted, rather than the eggs themselves.

A good guide to dating early egg cups is by the shape. Eighteenth century cups were shaped like hour-glasses. 'Breakfast-in-bed' sets were popular between about 1780 and 1820. These, in one

A selection of novelty egg cups.

piece, could take anything up to twelve eggs, toast in a rack, salt, a spoon, and sometimes there was a recess for a preserve. The Victorian period produced double egg cups, some with a large end for a goose egg and a smaller one for a hen's egg. For the rich there were special plates with recesses for quail eggs.

Children's novelty egg cups have featured such characters as Felix the cat, Bonzo the dog and, of course, a host of Disney animals.

A collector with an eye to profit should look for egg frames, and cups from the Coalport factory and designs by Clarice Cliff.

Walking Sticks

From the eighteenth century until the 1930s, the walking stick or cane was an indispensable accessory for any male within or on the fringe of fashion. Numerous theories have been put forward to explain its demise, one being its association with the army officer's swagger cane and a general sway from things military; another, that the cane was largely replaced by the umbrella, neatly rolled and used as part of the city worker's uniform. It is more likely the cane's decline has been simply due to the universal acceptance of the motor car as a means of transport in which a stick would be more an inconvenience than an asset.

Whatever the reason, the walking stick or cane is rapidly becoming obsolete, remaining in use almost entirely by the elderly and infirm. They are much more collector's items than utilitarian objects, though the collecting aspect is in its infancy and it is still possible to buy at reasonable prices. Those with gold or silver mounts are, understandably, expensive but plainer and still interesting sticks do not fetch high prices at auctions or in secondhand shops and are well worth picking up as an investment.

Eighteenth century canes, particularly those of French origin, were considerably longer in the stock than successive examples and were held by the shaft and not by the handle. The idea of the walking stick was obviously inspired by the pilgrim's or traveller's staff which was carried for defence and protection as well as for support.

It is, of course, the 'novelty' cane that is sought after by collectors; canes with snuff boxes in the top, those with a compartment for sovereigns, and some that disguise long thin spirit flasks. At the 1851 Great Exhibition in London was shown 'an astounding invention by Dr James Gray of Perth. He had designed a medical walking staff, which contained an enema, a catheter, a test-tube and test paper, a pair of forceps, a number of wax matches, and a pill box, divided, containing in each division, pills of various medicines'.

Sword sticks have mixed appeal, for both stick collectors and arms enthusiasts. Contrary to popular belief, it is not in itself illegal to buy or own sword sticks. It is left to the discretion of the police to decide if a carried sword stick constitutes an 'offensive weapon' under the Prevention of Crime Act, 1953.

Cameras

There is a collector known to the author who makes a reasonable profit each year by buying box and folding cameras to form a collection, and, once a year, putting them up for auction in a London sale room. The cameras this gentleman specializes in are of vintages between the early years of this century and the mid-1960s. But the days of this kind of investment may well be numbered as junk shop prices soar and as the collectors of this type of apparatus grow in number. It was only a very few years ago that wooden plate cameras could be purchased for only a few pounds, in

Sanderson camera, *c.* 1900.

Ensign 'Klito' double extension camera.

fact as cheaply as the Autograph Kodaks today. That time has gone and the wooden bodied plate cameras are not the attractive investment proposition they were. Early box cameras can still be acquired at attractive prices but this cannot last for long and collectors would be well advised to act fast.

The current bonanza in this field is for all Leica cameras and equipment made from the time of their introduction in 1924 by the Leitz Company of Wetzler, Germany, and this boom is likely to spread to other 'fashionable' vintage makes of 35-mm. miniatures. The original 35-mm. cameras were the Tourist Multiple and the Simplex Multi-Exposure, both American produced in 1914. Acquisition of either of these models would indeed be a prize.

Matchboxes and Booklet Matches

Collecting matchbox labels was first noted in France as early as 1859, when the term *Vulcanites* was given to these enthusiasts. It is now such a recognized activity that there was some doubt about including it in this book, the main purpose of which is to suggest more or less new and unusual subjects for collectors. If collecting for the future is to be recommended in this sector it would have to be directed at the enormous range of publicity booklet matches which abound at the present time, many of short manufacturing runs, and well worth collecting as trade ephemera.

Booklet matches were patented in 1892 by Joshua Pusey, an attorney at law of Lima, Pennsylvannia, and were manufactured from 1896 by the Diamond Match Company of Barberton, Ohio, who opened a British factory in 1899. About the year 1898 booklet matches were beginning to be recognised as a useful publicity medium. One of the first for this purpose being made by Diamond for the Mendelson Opera Company; now a prized collectors' piece.

Bottles

Bottles and Pot Lids, together with other products of Victorian and Edwardian rubbish dumps, are considered as typical of tomorrow's collectables. Certainly there have been many books published and each weekend hundreds, if not thousands, of treasure hunters set out on dump-digging excavations. It is this large number that raises doubts about the soundness of this sector of collecting when looked at from a profit-making viewpoint. Who knows the volume of now considered rare bottles and pot lids that will be excavated by these enthusiasts? Prices may still be high but already dealers are showing reluctance to buy as their stocks are becoming slow to move.

Soda syphons (*left*).

Earthen-ware bottles (*right*).

Of course, anything that costs nothing or, in this case, just the effort of digging and finding must be worth having but the indications are that the high prices of the moment cannot be sustained, and it may save disappointment if treasure hunters would think of their finds as material for their own collections or to be swopped with other enthusiasts rather than as money in the bank.

One of the useful things this treasure hunting craze has done is to bring to light some long-forgotten products. For instance, the unearthing of a bottle embossed with the words VALENTINE'S MEAT JUICES recently sparked off searches through the archives of surviving meat extract companies. Up to the time of writing this book, the bottle's origin remained a mystery.

Some bottle collectors specialize. The choice may be for inks, Codd or Hamiltons, medicinal, or even milk bottles. In view of the very real possibility of plastic or paper milk containers taking the place of glass bottles, the collecting of milk bottles may not be such a bad idea.

Milk bottles have their origin in the United States, dating back to 1879 when the Echo Farms Dairy Company of New York started to sell in this way for the convenience of their customers.

In Britain the Express Dairy in 1884 carried out experiments involving selling milk in wired cap bottles, but they soon abandoned the trials because of the expense. It was not until 1906 that fresh milk was regularly sold in glass bottles by British dairies.

The cardboard discs that preceded the aluminium milk bottle caps are now collectable items of trade ephemera. Also sought after are the openers; Bakelite disc caps with a spike projecting from the centre. It is doubtful if anyone under the age of thirty, unless told, would know the purpose of these objects.

There is now considerable uniformity in milk bottle design and a serious collector seeking variety in modern examples would have to purchase them from one of the several companies specializing in the reclamation and return of empty bottles.

Miniature Shoes

Shoes have, for centuries, been linked with good luck and have been manufactured in many miniature forms: in glass, china, metal, and wood as love tokens. Larger examples in glass could be used for drinking from or as flower vases. China shoes were used as pin trays, and silver, pewter and brass shoes had pin cushions in the opening at the top. Small silver shoes were a traditional form of wedding cake decoration.

All kinds of ladies' footwear have been made in miniature: Turkish slippers made by Minton, babies' bootees, and all manner of contemporary footwear—a collection of which can make a representative museum of shoes.

Some of the earliest surviving examples are those made by French prisoners-of-war from Napoleonic times, carved in both wood and bone, and used as snuff boxes or to contain miniature sets of dominoes.

There is a pleasant story behind the famous Goss china baby shoe. It is said that when Queen Victoria as a baby was staying at Sidmouth, a local shoemaker was commissioned to make for her a pair of shoes. In fact, he made three shoes, the third being acquired by W. H. Goss as a model for their product.

Some ceramic shoes from illustrious factories like Coalport and Worcester achieve high prices at auctions, but in the main they can still be picked up cheaply from curio shops. It has not yet become a fully fledged collecting interest, though all the indications are that it will do so in the near future, and at least one book is in the course of preparation.

Further Collecting Suggestions:
Commemorative Items and Souvenirs (events and places)
Ebony Elephants
Modern Enamel
Whistles

2   Adopting Orphans

By 'orphan' is meant, in this context, what few 'respectable' antiques shops would willingly touch with a barge pole and, if and when they did, it would be something of a joke. Many of the subjects in subsequent chapters may also be put into this classification.

It would be folly if any attempt were made to change the *status quo*. Collectors of 'orphans' can find rich pickings from the upper-crust shops at lower prices than they would down market, simply because such items are something of an embarrassment in a shop that deals in fine art and antiques. They do turn up in these shops because it is a hard commercial world and a dealer sometimes has to buy lesser goods in order to acquire one particular 'fine' piece. It is then usual practice to shunt off the dross and junk to the next auction or to a friend or associate in Portobello Road where it will fetch a price and clear the 'posh' shop to everybody's satisfaction.

That is admittedly a naive simplification of what goes on but it is certainly possible to pick up bargain 'orphans' in what are, at first sight, unlikely places.

Minor Inventions and Gadgets

Satisfying subjects for collecting are the lesser inventions of men (or women) who are better known for work in other fields.

Hiram Steven Maxim was born in Maine, U.S.A. in 1840, and is best remembered for the Maxim machine-gun which he patented in 1883, the result, it is said, of a conversation with a fellow American some two years earlier. 'If you want to make a pile of money', he was advised, 'invent something that will enable these Europeans to cut each other's throats with greater facility!' From the gun Maxim made his fortune, not in European conflict but in the Russo-Japanese War.

Maxim also invented a smokeless powder resembling cordite, a method of manufacturing artillery from one solid piece of metal and, as a member of the ship-building concern of Vickers, Sons &

Maxim at Crayford, Kent, worked on the principles of powered flight before the Wright brothers success in a field at Kittyhawk. The British honoured Maxim with a knighthood in 1901 and the French made him a Chevalier of the Legion of Honour.

Among the sideline 'throwaway' inventions of Hiram Maxim was the *Pipe of Peace and Maxim Inhaler*. In the booklet which accompanied the appliance, written at the Hiram Experimental Laboratories, Dulwich Common, and dated 20 January 1910, Sir Hiram describes how he suffered from bronchial and throat infections and had visited all the European health resorts without relief.

> 'The larger apparatus of my invention, which I call the Pipe of Peace embodies, like the Maxim Inhaler, the principles of direct inhalation. The principle of both is perfectly simple, but the effect is simply perfect. In both of them medicated vapours—vapour of menthol in the Maxim Inhaler, vapour of compound essence of pine, compounded by myself, in the Pipe of Peace, are released, not just inside the teeth, but close to the throat. My knowledge of chemistry enabled me to compound an essence of pine free from the liability which all ordinary pine essence possess to set up coughing at the beginning.'

A colourful testimonial from the inventor's own hand.

Inventions and gadgets do not have to be the products of great minds to make them collectable. One object in the author's collection is a small plastic item that arrived when a Bettaware salesman knocked at the door one day to ask if the lady of the house needed any brushes. When told that she was not in he proffered this gift as a reminder of his call. It turned out to be a toothpaste tube winder that is intended to slip over the end of the tube to roll it up as the paste is used. Gadgets such as this, and the *Saturday Bazaar* newspaper advertisements are full of them, make an unusual and fascinating collection.

There is not much chance of acquiring one of the masterpieces of minor inventions: the device used by the Duke of Wellington to raise his hat without taking his hands from the reins while riding. Equally unlikely to turn up is the little clock/stamping machine made in the late nineteenth century and intended for strapping on to the rear of chickens to date and time stamp each egg as it was laid.

On the other hand, quite a few minor inventions from the 1920s and '30s are still to be found. For instance, a clockwork fly trap which involved a fly landing on a revolving cylinder and ending up in a cage. There have been mousetraps on the market to kill up to five mice at a time!

At the 1851 Great Exhibition, Madam Caplin of 58, Berners Street, Oxford Street, London, had a variety of 'corrective clothing' displayed on stand 570A. One intriguing idea was called the 'Reversotractor', designed to prevent children from standing on one leg.

At the same Exhibition, on the stand of Johnson & Company, 113, Regent Street, London, was a patent ventilating hat, the principle being, that air was admitted through a series of channels cut in thin cork, this fastened to the leather lining, with a valve fixed in the top of the crown which could be opened and closed at pleasure, to allow the perspiration to escape.

What must be the ultimate in minor inventions was the walking stick that could be converted to a step ladder in the event of meeting a mad dog. The author's long search for one of these stick ladders continues.

Tiles and Bricks

There is undoubtedly a very considerable interest in collecting decorative ceramic tiles and prices are such that one wonders if it is not too late to include tiles in this book. It is still possible to obtain bargains in this field, though certainly acquisition potential is considerably less than it was in the 1960s when the property developers were having a smashing time pulling down fine old Victorian buildings to replace them with uniform living coups. In those days a ten bob note handed to a demolition foreman would result in a generous stock of ceramic tiles. And didn't the dealers know it? Profits of several thousand per cent. were and are still being made from those salad days!

One of the foremost tile factories in Britain was that of Maw & Company who manufactured at Jackfield, near Ironbridge, Salop. In 1977 over two million tiles, many over one hundred years old, were found at the abandoned works. Some of these will find their way on to the market, and there is a plan to reopen the factory as a working museum using the original plaster moulds. This must surely result in a stabilizing of prices, which is a good thing for those who collect for interest and pleasure, but not so good for those who collect for profit.

More speculative but, nonetheless, a fair gamble, is the collecting of building bricks. Not so many years ago almost every centre of population had its own brick works, each with its particular style of bricks and brick works. Since World War II there has been a steady decline in the number of brickworks, with an accelerating trend towards large works standardization. It's certainly worthwhile to accumulate a collection of at least one of each type of brick encountered, and they do not look at all bad built into a 'dry' wall in the garden.

Mr Henry Holt of Rossendale started collecting bricks in 1965 when, while walking on a demolition site, he picked up a brick with the mark of E. Holt Brickworks which was active in Rossendale in the nineteenth century. Twelve years later his collection numbered over 900 fully documented specimens.

The Kansas Brick Society of America is, so far, the only known association entirely engaged in this interest.

Plastics

The idea of collecting objects made from plastics may seem strange to most people and even abhorrent to purists. Nevertheless, we have seen over the past decade or two an emergence of interest in Bakelite and other synthetic materials, and it is not unreasonable to expect that as the years go by other plastic materials of more recent origins will find a place in collections. Already we see signs of this in specialized collecting fields; toys, cameras and advertising materials, for instance.

We can go back to 1862 and the International Exhibition in London for the first indication of the synthetic world to come, when combs, boxes and penholders made from a compound of nitrocellulose, camphor and alcohol were displayed. The material went under the name Parkesine, the invention of Alexander Parkes. Later, in 1866, Parkes founded the Parkesine Company at Hackney Wick, London.

An almost identical thermoplastic material was patented by John Wesley Hyatt of Albany, New York, in June 1869, and was marketed under the trade name of Celluloid—a name that was to become universal for this type of material.

The disadvantage of Parkesine and Celluloid was that it was highly inflammable, and materials of this division of plastics have not been made for many years. Which, of course, makes articles made from them highly collectable. An attribute it shares with Bakelite products, a material invented in 1907 by a Belgian, Dr Leo Baekland. The first commercial applications were for electrical insulation components made by the Loando Company of New Jersey.

Hand Lamps and Cycle Lamps

There is no need to evangelize the cause of collecting oil burning and acetylene lamps. For some years there has been a cult associated with these two forms of illumination, but the electric hand lamp and torch have been sadly neglected. There are numerous interesting models, both ancient and modern, making an excellent collecting subject.

The story of the electric hand lamp started in 1891 with the production of a square 2-candlepower bull's eye lantern, weighing 2 lbs with battery, made by the Bristol Electric Lamp Company (England), the first production batch of forty going to the Bristol General Omnibus Company.

In 1898, the New York factory of the American Electric and Novelty Manufacturing Company produced a cardboard bodied tubular torch. It had metal ends and a brass reflector. The American Electric and Novelty Manufacturing Company later became the American Ever Ready Company.

The Ever Ready No. 1 Torch was introduced into England in 1900, when it was sold by the British Mutoscope and Biograph Company of London, selling at 1 shilling and 6 pence ($7\frac{1}{2}$ p).

Any of these early electric lamps would be a considerable prize for a collector, but it is not necessary to go back as far as the turn of the century to find gems in this class of collectable. The author's particular favourites are the Word War II Service issues made by Ever Ready and Lucas, and some of the A.R.P. Civil Defence patterns produced by the former company.

This is still an inexpensive field of collecting and one to be strongly recommended when space and budget are the main considerations.

The Davy Safety Lamp was invented by Sir Humphry Davy and tested at Hebburn Colliery in January 1816. Later that year it was manufactured by John Newman of London. The miner's lamp is one of the most complex subjects in this division of collecting with no work of reference about the many manufacturers and their

26

A range of handlamps.

active dates. At least we know that the first practical electric miner's lamp—the Swan Bulb Lamp invented by R. E. Crompton—was demonstrated at the Pleasley Colliery, Mansfield, Nottinghamshire, on 8 June 1881.

Blow Lamps

Allied to the collecting of hand lamps is the less obvious subject of blow lamps, those workhorse tools of plumbers and decorators. There have been innumerable makes and models of blow lamps from all over the world since the first workable oil vapour lamp was introduced in 1880. The only thing certain about the inventor is that he was of Swedish nationality; the several claimants include Max Sievert, C. R. Nyberg (Sievert's engineer), the Lindquist brothers, and Ludwig Holm. Whoever was the original inventor, blow lamps have been readily available since 1891.

27

Pencil Sharpeners

On 16 April 1978, the *Sunday Times Colour Magazine* had a feature of few words and a large colour picture of some of the novelty pencil sharpeners which form the 500 plus collection of Alan and Suzie Fuller of Streatham, London.

This is the first collection of novelty pencil sharpeners that has so far come to light but it certainly will not be the last. They are ideal things to collect and have all the ingredients to put them high on the list of subjects which come within the terms of reference of this book. They are small in size—important for small home dwellers, they exist in great variety in age, subject matter and material but foremost, they are cheap, ranging in price when new, from a few pence to a little over £1.

Pencil sharpeners are strongly recommended to any collector for tomorrow with a small home and even smaller budget.

Charity Flags

Charity flags have all the ingredients of a full-scale collecting trend. There is the compactness of postage stamps, with the associated ease of inexpensively exchanging items through the mail, they are also colourful, attractive and representative of social history.

Although it is fairly certain that street collections date from 8 October 1891—Lifeboat Day—there is some doubt as to when the first actual Flag Day was held. It is generally acknowledged to have been in the year 1914, around the outbreak of World War I. One of the most convincing claimants is that of the Belgian Relief Fund on 3 October 1914.

Probably the most famous of Flag Days is 11 November, when the British Legion sell artificial poppies in the streets of Britain, the first of which was launched in 1921.

Greeting Cards

Greeting cards engraved by John Thompson were available in London from 1829 and it would be akin to teaching grandmother to suck eggs to suggest that greeting cards make fascinating and even profitable collecting subjects. Valentines, World War I

Among the first postcards published to benefit U N I C.E.F. (founded 1946).

(Reverse of cards reads 'Theatrum Sanitas di Ububchasym de Baldach Biblioteca Casanatense di Roma, Italy'.)

'sweetheart' cards, and early Christmas cards, are all acknowledged collectables.

However, a comparatively neglected field is the Charity Christmas Card, the first of which was published for Christmas 1949 by U.N.I.C.E.F., and designed by seven-year-old Jitka Samkova of the village of Rudolfo, Czechoslovakia—a picture of children dancing round a maypole.

Charity cards have now taken a large percentage of the Christmas cards sold and a collection could become enormous. It is certainly necessary for a collector to specialize in say, certain years or group of charities.

Thermos Flasks

These appear to have been neglected by collectors over the years, presumably with the assumption that if you have seen one, you have seen the lot. But this is not true and vacuum flasks can be recommended to anyone with a pioneering instinct seeking a new

29

collecting field; possibly one that will grow considerably in the next few years.

It was in 1892 that the first vacuum flask was made in Cambridge, England, by James Dewar. The first model, in fact, still survives at the Royal Institution.

For twelve years the only uses that could be seen for the 'Dewar vessel', as it was understandably known, were in the laboratory but, in 1904, Reinhold Burger in Germany spotted its potential domestic use and offered a prize for the most appropriate name. The winning entry was 'thermos'—Greek for 'hot'—which became a protected brand name. The first manufactured Thermos flask could be produced at a rate of only eight a day by each skilled craftsman.

Prams

Close to the village of Biddenden in the heart of Kent, stands the ancient moated house of Bettenham Manor. Here Mr Jack Hampshire carries on his devotion; his self-appointed task of collecting and recording a form of wheeled vehicle the known history of which goes back about one hundred years before that of the practical motor car. Yet it is a form of transport which, until recently, has attracted little attention.

The vehicle in question is the pram or baby carriage. Antique collectors and dealers have been aware of the attraction of Victorian bassinets and mailcarts for a number of years but, as is pointed out to visitors to this, The Baby Carriage Collection, the coachbuilt pram is now virtually a thing of the past with only one or two companies still engaged in production. Their place on the pavements has been taken by the folding eight-wheeled push chair.

A study of the body styling and wheel arrangement of prams can be as intriguing as that of motor cars and there are at least as many varieties, from the 'reversible' with handles at both ends which eliminated the need for turning on narrow pavements, to the remarkable Dunkley Pramotor, 'The Greatest Attraction at the Motor Show, 1922.' It had a 1 hp 2-stroke motor with kick start, and a top speed of 5 m.p.h. The power unit, like a motor scooter without a front wheel, fitted behind the pram itself and the mother or nanny stood on foot rests on either side of the engine. The price was 100 guineas for a Pramotor with an 'all-weather body' (folding hood, adjustable windscreens and window), 150 guineas for a

A collection of baby carriages, 1845–1921

. . . and 1913–1950.

saloon body, and 35 guineas for the motor unit only which could be attached to any standard Dunkley pram. It is not known if any Pramotors survive but if one could be unearthed it would certainly be very rewarding to the finder.

3   Cutting a Niche

For anyone anxious to make a name, and enjoy the mixed blessings of appearing in the press, on television and radio, there is no easier way than by choosing a collecting subject that is unique, better still bizarre, or at the very least, unusual. There is also the danger of being known as a bit of a crackpot, but this is a risk worth taking if fame is the spur.

This is how it is done:

Select a collecting subject that, it seems, has been neglected, and make a start. Talk about it in pubs and at work and, with luck, donated articles will soon be arriving at the door to get the collection started. All known manufacturers of the product concerned should be contacted and made aware that the collection exists; they should be asked for company and product histories, and manufacturing processes.

At this point a certain expertise can be claimed, particularly if it is the first collection of this class of product! Photographs should be taken and an embryonic catalogue compiled. So armed, the friendly local newspaper reporter can then be contacted. He or she, always on the lookout for a good, if off-beat story, will get it into the local rag and, if it is a hungry or ambitious reporter, the story may find its way into one of the nationals.

Now is the time to work out an 'image'. Ideally, there should be fifty-five kids to support and/or a leaking roof and a wicked landlord, but here is this devoted collector carrying on regardless. Alternatively, the burnt matchsticks or whatever should be tagged with some social or historical importance. The prepared 'image' should sound convincing enough for when the letters start arriving and the telephone begins to ring.

Preferably the spouse of the collector should answer the phone—there are few better boosts to the ego within matrimony than to casually reply with an 'oh, yes' to the surprised observation that it is 'Jack Demanio on the phone, dear' or 'it's the Sunday Times Magazine for you.' Take them all on, but play it diplomatically, don't accept similar television programmes like *Blue Peter* and *Magpie*—that will only cause bad feelings all round.

Do all the television and radio work offered. It's great fun and the former pays well. You will probably be scared but don't worry too much. The result is always far better than was thought possible, and this is the start of a professional career as a collector.

Notes of caution:

Beware of the 'feedback' and the taxman; the latter will have a note of what fees you have received, and the 'feedback' letters will be numerous—they always are—and sometimes they can be tear-jerking: 'I am an old age pensioner and have in my possession one of those things like yours shown on the telly, but mine is in much better condition. Times are hard and I am wondering how much it is worth or how much you will give me for it.'

It is not within the scope of this book to instruct on how to reply to the 'feedback' mail, nor how to answer any publisher's enquiries about a possible book from you on this unusual collecting theme. Some little secrets must be kept!

Here are a few suggestions for collecting subjects that would cut their own niche. Of course, these recommendations are self-defeating as, for starters, the media does not want more than one collector for each subject and, hopefully, this book will be read so widely that there will be hundreds of collections growing up, like daisies after the rain, covering everything that is mentioned through the chapters.

Electrical Appliances

The 1970s have seen the birth of a new collecting interest: electric light bulbs. This is not really surprising as the potential scope is enormous. Two types of incandescent electric lamps first appeared almost simultaneously but were developed independently by Thomas Alva Edison, Menlo Park, New Jersey, and by Joseph Swan, Newcastle-upon-Tyne, England. Production began in the U.S.A. by the Edison Electric Lamp Works in 1880 and, in Britain, by the Swan Electric Light Company in 1881. Initially, prices were $2.50 and 25 shillings respectively.

It is not suggested that collectors should seriously consider vintage electric washing machines; important though these machines are in the history of industry and effect on social

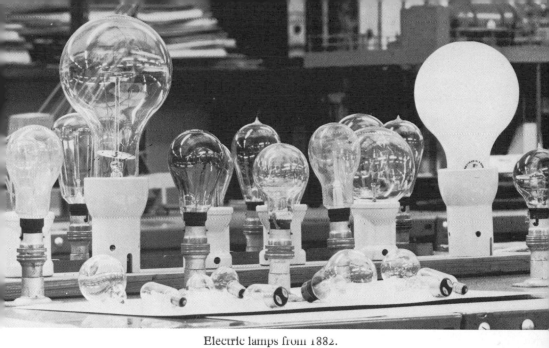

Electric lamps from 1882.

Heating appliances, 1912–1930.

conditions. These are perhaps better left to specialist museums. In this connexion it may amuse the reader if the author recounts an incident which could be considered as a cautionary tale.

One Saturday morning in the early 1970s there was a knock at the front door. The callers explained that they were trying to dispose of a late 1920s Canadian Beatty washing machine that had been owned by a recently deceased aunt. Attempts had been made to donate the machine to the London Science Museum but they had turned it down as there was already a similar example on display. The author, of course, ever ready to preserve vintage machinery of any kind, willingly accepted the Beatty, hoping it would be possible to find a home for it at the then newly established Milne Museum of the South Eastern Electricity Board. This was not to be as, like the Science Museum, the Milne already had one. So there the monster stands incongruously displaying itself in the library. Surely the last word in conversation pieces!

The same note of caution must be given about electric cookers, but nevertheless there are a small number of electric appliance collectors, most of them with a commercial interest in hiring to film and television companies.

An electric cooker for commercial sale was first made by the Carpenter Electric Heating Company of St Paul, Minnesota, in 1891. It had an oven, 18 ins long, 14 ins high and 12 ins deep, made from white pine and lined with asbestos, felt and tin. There were glass panels in the doors so that the progress of the cooking could be observed—a feature that reappeared on electric ovens in the late 1950s.

Two years later, 1893, Crompton & Company produced an electric oven at Chelmsford, Essex, and in four years had extended their range to three models priced between £10 and £16 and a table model with hot-plate for £5 10 shillings (£5.50). Early electric cookers are comparatively rare, gas being a considerably cheaper means of heating food. There were only some 75,000 electric cookers in service in Britain in 1930, after which the number grew rapidly. To find a pre-1930 vintage electric cooker should make the day for any domestic appliance collector.

Much more convenient to collect are the smaller electrical appliances, and those made before the recent safety regulations are rare.

Electric radiators were early in their appearance, the first being in 1889, made by the Burton Electric Company of Richmond,

Virginia. These early radiators were shaped like a low cast-iron table on iron legs and they were first used on electric tramcars. In Britain, Crompton & Company of Chelmsford sold iron screen radiators from 1894.

Probably the earliest electrical appliance that can be expected to come to light when hunting for such things would be an electric bell, the first recorded invention of which was by Joseph Henry of Albany, New York, in 1831.

Americans certainly figure prominently in the history of invention of domestic appliances. Henry W. Seely of New York first patented an electric iron in 1882. It was not until ten years later that the British company of J. J. Dowsing demonstrated their first electric iron at the Crystal Palace.

Sharing with the electric iron the year 1882 as its year of invention, is the electric fan, the first being a two-bladed disc fan made by the Crocker & Curtis Electric Company of New York. In Britain, B. Verity & Company, London, made fans from about 1888.

1891 was the year of introduction of the electric kettle, first produced by the Carpenter Electric Manufacturing Company of St Paul, Minnesota.

Among all this American pioneering work the British manufacturer, Crompton, can claim to be the first maker of an electric toaster in 1893.

Gas Appliances

For long ancestry, gas appliances beat those of electricity by a considerable period— the practical starting point being when William Murdoch lighted his offices and house at Redruth, Cornwall, with coal gas in 1792. Seven years later Philippe Leben of Bruchay, near Joinville, France, patented a combined lamp and heater called the 'Thermolampe', which was demonstrated in 1800 at the Hotel Seignelay, Paris. The inventor, by the way, met an untimely death on Napoleon's Coronation Day in 1804, when he was stabbed on the Champs Elysées.

Gas was quickly accepted for lighting and heating, from 1836 gas cookers for domestic use were available, made by James Sharp at a factory in Northampton. In 1852, the 'modern' form of cooker, with an oven and cooking shelves, was produced under the name Bower's Registered Gas Cooking Stove.

The company of Pettit & Smith produced, in 1856, a gas fire

Appliances from the Davis Gas Stove Co. Ltd., 1901.

based on the principle of the Bunsen burner. Later in 1885, the gas mantle was patented by Carl Auer von Welsbach, an Austro-Hungarian, who had worked with Bunsen.

With the use of gas now confined almost exclusively to cooking and heating, any articles connected with gas lighting are becoming increasingly rare and collectable.

Barbed Wire and Cordage

The motive behind the barbed wire collecting movement in the U.S.A. seems, to many of us brought up on more conventional collecting themes, to be obscure. But to the Americans barbed wire is as much a part of social history as say, rural cottage industry tools are to the British. Without barbed wire it would have been hard indeed to enclose the great cattle ranches.

A patent covering barbed wire was granted to Lucien B. Smith of Kent, Ohio, on 25 June 1867. This was a complex product using wire spiked blocks of wood threaded on the main wire strand. Collectors have long been seeking an example of Smith's wire but, as far as is known, without success. It must be doubted if it was ever put into production.

In the following year, 1868, a patent for what was advertised as 'strong thorney hedge' was granted to M. Kelly. It was known as Kelly's Diamond because of the shape of the barbs twisted in the main strand. Some fences of this type of wire are still standing.

Serious collectors have listed over 1,500 types of barbed wire.

It might be difficult to work up much enthusiasm for scratchy, tearing fencing, particularly as we in Europe are naturally inclined to associate barbed wire with the mud and horror of Flanders fields in World War I. What would seem a more pleasant and certainly more gentle subject for collectors is cordage. Rope and string, over the years, has been produced in a range of sizes and materials that offers the biggest possible challenge to cataloguers. It is not unreasonable to predict that cordage will become collectable. Apart from its appeal of challenge, a collection of 18 ins lengths (the standard adopted by barbed wire collectors) would look quite attractive.

Soap

When one becomes known as an *avant garde* collector, especially where social and industrial history is concerned, some of the perks or crosses to bear (depending on how one looks at it) are the 'consultancies'. The letter box is full every morning with letters that all too often end '. . . how much is it worth?' Those that end '. . . . can you tell me something about it?' are much nicer to receive as, apart from boosting the ego, they are good incentive to delve and uncover some facts that would otherwise remain at the bottom of the priority pile. If there is a small fee for the consultancy, so much the better.

Most newspapers have a panel of specialized consultants they can approach for answers to letters received through their correspondence columns and most specialized collectors find themselves rung up for advice on how a reply can be given. At times the volume of these enquiries makes one think that the job is more that of a journalist than a collector. Yes, dear reader, all this and more can be yours if you follow the trail of the unusual.

For his sins, the author acts as a consultant on industrial history subjects to a national daily letter column which prides itself in being able to answer most questions on almost every subject. It is a great challenge and there is gloom in the household when a question defies all attempts to find an answer or even to hazard a guess at one.

On a particularly memorable morning, sixty-seven letters arrived from this source; among them was one from a lady in south east London who had come across a wrapped bar of soap marked 'Household Soap $\frac{1}{4}$d'. For the benefit of the young, $\frac{1}{4}$d stands for one farthing, or quarter of one old penny, or one tenth of a penny in the present coinage. The enquirer wanted to know its date and who made it. As with tea and some other household commodities the quickest and often the most reliable indication for dating is by price, but in this case there was a difficulty; even by Victorian standards this bar was far too cheap. In the 1880s the average price of household soap was 8d per pound weight and, before the soap tax was taken off in England in the late 1860s it was even higher.

The Industrial Chemicals Department of the Science Museum in London were unable to help in spite of their quite delightful collection of Victorian soap in a showcase on the second floor. It was suggested it was, perhaps, made by a company later taken over by the Unilever empire, but here again we drew a blank, with the lady who keeps the archives there denying any knowledge of such a priced product.

This was not the most successful of researches and the

conclusion was that it was made by some small cut-price company sometime in the 1870s.

What this story does show is that soap could be a 'star' collectable. Surviving pieces are rare as most of it is used. It is durable and is a pretty good reflection of social history. Certainly there is scope here for some in depth research. Soap can be strongly recommended to anyone wanting to 'cut a niche' in an unusual and possibly important collecting field.

Further Collecting Suggestions:
  Artificial Flowers
  Clothes Hangers
  Colour Swatches

4

Themes

There are several alternative foundations on which a collection can be based. One is 'period' and justification for this kind of collecting has been attempted in the chapter entitled 'Time Capsules'. Then there is the most popular form of collecting, that of like objects, be they stamps, sewing machines, coins or motor cars.

Thirdly, there is theme collecting, when the aim is to assemble items of different types and functions but linked by some common thread; the kind of collection we might expect to see in a local history museum.

The theme that springs to mind as being ripe for exploitation and one that would make an ideal subject for a new specialized museum, either privately owned or sponsored, is that of Air Raid Precautions—Civil Defence. The author has long wanted to be connected with the establishment of such a museum, having had some small experience of A.R.P and A.F.S. (Auxiliary Fire Service) in the early part of World War II, but up to now neither time or outside co-operation have been found. More about this later.

Office Machines

With the centenary production year in 1975, typewriters at least, among items of office machinery, have become acknowledged collectables, much to the amusement of some of us who have been indulging ourselves in daily use of vintage machines for years. They are now acknowledged to an extent that makes it unnecessary to dwell on typewriters in this book, which is concerned with more obscure collecting ideas.

Other office machines have not yet had the same following and it seems appropriate to give more space to a neglected office servant, the copier or duplicator.

Stencil duplicating is so commonplace that it is now hard to believe there could be anything exciting or dramatic about it. It was, nevertheless, a great invention—a copying machine was so fundamentally different from anything that had been known before that it completely revolutionized the late nineteenth century office. It was so simple, and the invention spread through the world with astonishing speed.

Even up to the end of the nineteenth century, the office clerk was hunched on his high stool, laboriously copying business correspondence. The copying clerk was cheap and attempts to replace him with a more efficient copying process met with little success.

A notable attempt was made by James Watt, better known for his work on the steam engine. He devised a copy press and a patent was granted to him in February 1780. Letter copiers based on Watt's patent were in common use until World War I, when carbon paper became universally available.

Watt's process made use of a special ink in which the document to be copied was written. The document was then placed in contact with a dampened sheet of unsized tissue paper and rolled in a mangle type press. Under pressure, the ink of the original was transferred to the tissue. The impression so obtained was, of course, in reverse, but the paper was thin enough to permit the image to be read from the back. It was a slow process and the press was heavy to operate.

In 1875 Thomas Alva Edison was transmitting Morse signals by the use of perforations in paper strips—an invention that was instrumental in the discovery of the talking machine or *phonograph*—and a number of Edison's patents of this time show he was thinking along the lines of using this process in a form of stencil duplicating. But Edison's attempts were crude and the perforating instrument too heavy and cumbersome to handle.

David Gestetner was a young stockbroker's clerk from Csorna, Hungary who, after a financial collapse in Vienna, emigrated to the United States with no assets other than an alert, inventive mind and a preoccupation with copying—acquired during his early clerical days. Selling Japanese kites on a street corner in Chicago to earn a meagre living he noticed the peculiar qualities of the paper from which they were made. It was light yet strong and coated with wax to make it waterproof.

Gestetner found the means of travelling to Britain and, in 1881, took out a British patent covering a new kind of implement for writing on a sheet of waxed paper. This 'pen' had, in place of the conventional nib, a tiny revolving wheel. The stencil waxed paper

Roneo No. 5 Duplicator, *c.* 1904.

sheet was placed on a smooth hard surface and written on with the special pen which pierced the stencil as the wheel revolved.

The invention was called the 'Cyclostyle Pen' and marked the beginning of stencil duplicating as an efficient, commercially practical process.

Flatbed duplicators, stemming from David Gestetner's 'Cyclostyle', can still be found in junk shops at give away prices. One can always make a duplicator a 'conversation piece', telling visiting friends about one's original 'Cyclostyle' or 'Neo-Cyclostyle' and astounding them with the useless information that the stencil is the same sort of paper that the Japanese have, for centuries, used on their fighting kites!

Rotary duplicators appeared first in 1901, from both Gestetner and from the newly formed company of RoNeo (the name made up from the words 'rotary' and 'neostyle'). Like the flatbeds, early rotary duplicators can be picked up very cheaply and are certainly well worth collecting.

The envelope addressing machine is a refinement of the duplicator and no office machine collection should be without at least one example of a RoNeo or one made by the Elliot Addressing Machine Company of Cambridge, Massachusetts; both venerable *marques* in this field.

The first sign that the reign of the duplicator was coming to an end came on 22 October 1938, when Chester F. Carlson of Pittsford, New York, patented his invention of a successful Xerox

Bulky but certainly collectable pieces of office equipment.

copying machine. But the world had to wait until 1950 before such a machine could be bought, manufactured by the Haloid Company of Rochester, New York, and it was as late as 1957 before Rank Xerox produced the first British-built machine; The Times Publishing Company having to pay £1,250 for the privilege of owning the first production example.

Photocopiers are perhaps too large for most collectors. For them there could be a worse decision than to concentrate on calculating machines. Their origins are deeply set in history, the earliest example being that of the abacus with which eastern peoples can make calculations with remarkable speed.

The first recorded mechanical adding machine was built in 1623 by Wilhelm Schickard in Tübingen, Germany. But what is probably the most famous calculating machine of all time is that of Blaise Pascal, whose father was a clerk making hundreds of calculations a day in the course of his work. It was to make his father's life easier that Pascal invented a calculating machine. In principle it was simple; its refinement being a clutch device or *sautoir* which 'made it as easy to add 1 to 999 as to 1'. According to his sister, Pascal invented the machine in 1642, when he was 19 years old. Some seventy machines were built, some as presents for the French monarch. It must be remembered that this was not purely a decimal counter; the French at that time used *deniers* and *sous*—twelfths and twentieths of a franc.

There are examples of early and beautifully built calculators from the eighteenth and nineteenth centuries. Of course, these are real treasures of collecting and they command very high prices. Such a machine is the Arithometre made by Thomas de Colmar of Paris around 1850; a machine capable of all the processes of addition, subtraction, multiplication and division. One surviving example in a private collection is set in a beautifully veneered cabinet, approximately 24 ins long, decorated and reinforced with brass inlays. It carries a serial number of 1043, which suggests that a substantial number were made.

Machines like this must be regarded as scientific and mathematical instruments but they were the forerunners of the first commercial calculators that appeared in the 1880s; one operated by a keyboard being marketed by Door, Felt of Chicago, their first sale being to the Equitable Gas Light and Fuel Company. The Felt & Tarrant Manufacturing Company, also of Chicago, made the first machine that would actually record the figures on paper, the

Comptographer. This and the 'non-recording' Comtometer remained in production, with modifications, for many years.

It would be a mistake to dismiss miniaturized pocket calculators when considering a future collectable. Like transistorized radio sets, pocket calculators are made in such numbers and at such prices as to cause them to be expendable when they go wrong. Already calculators of about seven years old have become hard to find.

Of the smaller items of office equipment, rubber stamps (first produced by John Leighton of London in 1864), stapling machines and punches are all worth more than a passing thought.

Household Gadgets and Machines

It is refreshing in these days of radical change, to find an item of machinery that may be bought new in a shop, and made to a design that has been substantially unchanged for the past 100 years. This

Items of small domestic equipment from *c.* 1920–1930.

Cast-iron holloware—pots and pans—make an interesting collection. *From left to right*: glue pot, first made in 1836; 'digester' (an early form of pressure cooker) made from 1836–1937; oven-to-table casserole first made in 1956.

The white vitreous enamel mincer in the centre of the picture is one of the first ever made (in about 1896). On the left is a 1930's type which was available for 3 shillings in 1937. A mincer made for Sweden is pictured on the right.

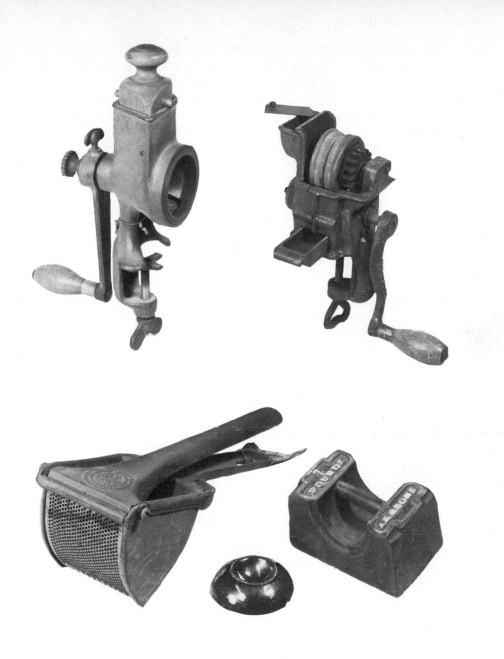

Vegetable slicer 1911 (*top left*), Knife cleaner 1890–1910 (*top right*),
potato masher 1888–1957, poker stand 1957, and bar weight 1873–1912.

is the Spong coffee mill. The present day catalogue quotes the mill as having 'large deep-cut grinding cones adjustable for fineness. The mill may be screwed to the wall or clamped to the table. All clamps are hinged to save space.' Early twentieth century Spong catalogues show a very similar machine, the main differences being a bent cranking handle and a non-folding table clamp.

Coffee mill designs are noted for their long life, much to the pleasure of those indulging in nostalgia but to the slight inconvenience of those who try to date the things. French made Peugeot mills are notoriously difficult in this regard.

To get back to Spong, one of the *grandes marques* of British domestic ironmongery, which was founded in 1856 by J. O. Spong. There is a 'landmark' that will help in dating Spong appliances: the company became limited on 18 January 1909, and any product made after that date will be so marked. Spong, with Kent (who exhibited at the 1851 Great Exhibition) and Vono, were the chief makes of rotary knife cleaners sold in Britain until the 1930s. Spong ceased production of these in 1938. Rotary knife cleaners are now ridiculously highly priced and are not recommended for investment collecting as it is hard to see how the prices can increase much more.

This does not apply to food mincing machines which are still to be found at give away prices in junk shops. Again Spong figure strongly as makers of mincers, as do the Enterprise Manufacturing Company of Philadelphia who were advertising their 'meat choppers' at least as early as 1855, priced at $2. It is still possible to buy them at less than this price, but it is hard to predict the future trend.

In 1975, Spong published a reprint of one of their late nineteenth century catalogues, and fascinating reading it makes with the amazingly diverse range of products: sausage and general mincing machines, including one called the 'Monster' weighing 'about 11 cwt', coffee mills, sausage fillers, cask stands, mixers, meat slicers, bread cutters, knife cleaners, fire extinguishers, fire balls made from 'pure india rubber', fire escapes, freezers, gas burners or 'utilizers', portable shampoos 'for summer and winter use', corner weights for carpets, 'Koh-i-noor' advertising medium that flashes gas, electric or paraffin light, rat traps, and ice chests. It is all straight forward gadgetry but emphasizes the range of collectables in the domestic field. As late as the end of the 1960s, all the items in this catalogue, with the exception of the 'Koh-i-noor' would have been considered so much rubbish; the author recalling the purchase of a Victorian ice chest for five shillings (25 p) in 1970. It is certainly different in the late 1970s, and it is fairly safe to forecast that domestic equipment of almost any age will be a good and steadily appreciating investment.

Other domestic appliances worth seeking are: pressure cookers (invented in 1680 by a London residing Frenchman, Denis Papin), automatic tea-makers (first made by Fred Clarke of Birmingham, England in 1902), and wall-mounted can openers (marketed from 1927, at first by the United States Manufacturing Company, St Louis).

In fact, can openers of all kinds and of all dates of origin are predicted to be important collectors' items of tomorrow, reaching the status now held by corkscrews and other bottle opening devices. Early cans of food, which started to appear in the 1820s, carried the instruction: Cut round on the top with a chisel and

Irons powered variously: asbestos sleeve iron (*top left*); modern Portuguese charcoal iron (*top right*); 'O.K.' gas iron (*centre*); 'Brilliant' spirit iron (*bottom left*); U.S. carbide acetylene gas iron.

hammer'. Cans of that period were of heavy iron and it was only when thinner steel cans, with a rim round the top, came into use in the 1860s could there be inspiration to invent a can opener. Little is known about the early devices which were probably quite complicated mechanisms with which a shopkeeper could open a can before handing it over to the customer. Much research work needs to be done before we know the history of these early can openers.

In England the first appearance of a *domestic* can opener was in the 1880s. This was of the bull's head type—for 'bully beef'. Can opening devices—even those of recent origin—have a fascination of their own and there is a good opportunity for collectors to make a valuable contribution to industrial history research.

Another recommendation in the domestic field is bread boards and knives. They are attractive in display and are already receiving some attention from collectors. Like all treen, they are remarkably hard to date and it comes down to a matter of intuition. However, at today's fairly low prices it would be difficult to go far wrong.

Cleaning Machines

Before the invention of mechanical aids, the only means available to housewives and servants for cleaning carpets was to hang them on a clothes line and beat them. It was not a pleasant job. There was all the dust to settle on the unfortunate person and perhaps to flow back in the house. Eventually a mechanical cleaner that could ease the housewives' burden had to to be invented.

In 1811, James Hume was granted a patent covering mechanical sweeping but it was not until 1842 that any practical cleaning device was conceived. This, the invention of Sir Joseph Whitworth, was a well-engineered device designed for street cleaning. An endless chain of brushes, driven from the axle of a cart, carried dirt into a container. This idea was applied some sixteen years later to mechanical carpet sweeping by revolving brushes, operated by the wheels of the device when pushed over the carpet.

Around 1858 arrived the first crude uses of air for carpet cleaning. One American device used a four-bladed fan, employed lengthways like a revolving brush and driven from wheels pushed over the carpet, to blow dust into a container. Another idea consisted of revolving brushes combined with an air current

Sixty years of Hoover. This is one of the earliest, pre-World War I models.

And here is one of the sophisticated models of today—an easier starting-point for a collection perhaps.

53

provided by bellows driven by a connecting rod attached to the wheels.

None of these inventions were really effective or popular. Even as late as 1875 *The Manual of Domestic Economy Suited to Families Spending from £150 to £1500 a Year* recommended: 'to dust carpets and floors: sprinkle tea-leaves on them, then sweep them carefully. Fine carpets should be gently done, on the knees. Those parts that are most soiled may be scrubbed with a small hand brush when it is not considered necessary to undertake a general washing of the whole; always adding a little gall to the water to preserve the colours.'

A breakthrough came in 1876, when the owner of a china shop in Grand Rapids, Michigan, Melville R. Bissell, fed up with headaches and sneezing attacks caused by the dusty straw from the packing cases, solved his problem by inventing a sweeper with revolving brushes, adjustable to variations in floor surfaces. This became the 10 shilling sweeper—the Bissell 'Grand Rapids' produced by the Bissell Carpet Sweeping Company.

Carpet sweepers can form an interesting collection. There are still many wooden-bodied Bissell and Ewbank sweepers around which cost less than £1 in junk shops. The pleasing thing about these pieces of domestic machinery is that it is difficult to find two that are exactly alike: wheels, tyres, bumpers, handle, frame, and transfer differences, are the points to note. A collection of sweepers can go back to the 1870s and can be open-ended as a few modern metal and plastic examples make interesting comparisons.

Manually-operated domestic suction cleaners were developed and manufactured in the closing years of the nineteenth century—some pumped by hand, some by foot, and, at least one, by the wheel of the machine. This last invention had the refinement of a water filter to absorb the dirt. Many of these suction cleaners needed two or more housemaids to operate them.

Meanwhile, inventive minds went on working at the problem of developing cleaning methods. Compressed air was used in foundries to blow dust from castings, and then—at the end of the century—for general cleaning.

In considering the developments of domestic appliances in general and suction cleaners in particular, it is impossible to over-estimate the effect of the electric motor, which had been invented as early as 1821 and was already used in transport towards the end of the nineteenth century and, from then, its use spread rapidly to every conceivable purpose, including the motive force for suction cleaners.

Soon after the turn of the century, the earliest mechanical (as opposed to manual) suction cleaner was invented. This must be credited to Hubert Booth, a builder of bridges and Ferris wheels, including those at Blackpool and Vienna. The story goes that Booth was attending a demonstration of a blower type cleaner for railway carriages at St Pancras station (another version of the tale gives the venue as a music hall, but it matters not), when he suggested that sucking rather than blowing would be more effective, but was told that his idea had been tried and found wanting. He went home—it is said—lay on the floor and drew dust from the carpet through his handkerchief with his mouth, thereby working out the principle of the first viable mechanical suction cleaner.

The Vacuum Cleaner Company Limited was formed in Victoria Street, London, and machines built to Booth's patent. These were large horse-drawn contraptions which sucked dirt from houses and business premises through hose pipes. A great disadvantage of these machines was that the noise of the motor caused horses to bolt, which pleased neither police nor population.

In 1907 occurred the event of the utmost significance in the development of domestic suction cleaning. This was the introduction of the first Hoover cleaner at North Canton, Ohio, manufactured and marketed by W. H. Hoover. The maker was a well-known leather manufacturer but, with the popular reception of the Hoover cleaner, the business was turned entirely to the production of domestic appliances. The first Hoover cleaners, though crude by today's standards, were recognizable ancestors of the suction cleaners produced since then.

So far, the collecting of suction cleaners has been confined to museums of technology but, with the acceleration in the mechanical collecting field, it seems likely that one day electric cleaners will be featuring at specialist sales. Already people are paying fairly high prices for manual suction cleaners such as Daisy, Zedel and Star, but the names of Tellus, Hoover and Electrolux are comparatively unknown in the Sales and Wants columns. They deserve more attention.

The photographs on page 53 reveal an interesting comparison between one of the earlier Hoover models produced before World War I and one on sale in the late 1960s.

A fascinating group of hinges, from the merely functional to the highly ornate.

Ornamental design in cast iron: trivets, gothic latch, letter plates, Queen Victoria and paperweight 1871–c. 1899.

Small Ironmongery

Wood screws, or screw nails as they are sometimes called in the U.S.A., have an interesting history and are well worth the attention of collectors.

It was in the sixteenth century that gunsmiths and armourers started using a small tool with a blade—the original screwdriver—to adjust the firearm mechanisms. These metal parts were fixed to the gun stock with nails that had a twist in the spike. Hammered in, they were extremely difficult to remove. A solution was found by cutting a slot in the nailhead before they were hammered home, so that they could be turned and removed with a 'turnscrew'.

The early twisted nails were hand made and expensive, but towards the end of the eighteenth century they began to be machine made by Birmingham manufacturers. These were cheap enough to be used for fixing hinges, doors and furniture, and about the year 1780, the long-bladed 'London-pattern' screwdriver was introduced.

Until about 1840, wood screws were blunt but then Nettlefold pointed wood screws were first made, the forerunners of the modern designs of screws.

Collecting examples of screws of various periods is not difficult and most antique furniture restorers will help specialist collectors.

Strangely, nuts and bolts are older in origin than woodscrews, and indeed, were perfected by 1550. Box spanners surviving from the seventeenth century are relatively common, and it should not be beyond an enthusiast's ingenuity to establish a collection of spanners and their related nuts and bolts ranging from an early period to the present day.

Keys may conveniently be included under 'small ironmongery', though specialist collectors in this field may find such grouping as unacceptable. It is a trend among key collectors to acquire keys for their usage associations rather than for their manufacturing origins. A few years ago some keys from the Garland Collection came on the market, including keys from the Royal Albert Hall, Lord's Cricket Ground, Greenwich Royal Observatory, Crystal Palace, Drury Lane Theatre, Biograph Cinema at Victoria, Newgate Prison, Imperial Airways Hangar of Croydon Aerodrome, Davis Theatre at Cambridge, Cambridge University, the 'Titanic', Argyll Theatre at Birkenhead, Leeds City of Varieties Music Hall, Urquhart Castle, Carlisle Castle and Taunton

Railway Station. A selection to appeal to any taste!

Collecting modern keys from famous buildings may well be a rewarding interest. Locks are often changed for security reasons and, with a little perseverance, it is not too difficult to acquire such keys through contacts with locksmiths.

The Yale lock, by the way, is considerably older than is generally realised, being patented by Linus Yale of Newport, New York, on 6 May 1851.

A.R.P.—Civil Defence

As indicated at the opening of this chapter, there is one collecting theme that is simply crying out for followers and even a specialized museum—that of A.R.P. and Civil Defence items. Though London's Imperial War Museum and the Warnham War Museum, near Horsham, Sussex, have both devoted divisions to Air Raid Precautions and there are various exhibits in museums of towns that were subjected to war-time air attack, there is a serious need for a strong central collection.

A display of A.R.P. equipment.

The more common paraphernalia of gas masks (more correctly and officially known in war-time as respirators) and steel helmets are being bought from junk shops by collectors, but there was such a mass and variety of equipment for civilian defence in Britain during World War II, it would need a bevy of knowledgeable dealers and collectors to stabilize the market. The field is wide open for exploitation.

If we were to research from the beginning we would have to start in June 1915, when the first uniformed civilian defence unit was formed in World War I, the Architectural Association Air Raid Section. Research into this body would call for long and painstaking work and, for most, it would be more convenient to start in 1937–8, when the A.R.P. Air Raid Warden service was formed, each of its members being issued with a real silver badge, an armband, a torch, steel helmet, 'CD' (Civilian Duty) respirator, 'Acme Thunderer' whistle (to blow an air raid alarm in case the sirens failed), and a long cane with a bulldog clip on the end to hold gas detector papers for dipping into puddles suspected of containing liquid mustard gas. Three sizes of 'Civilian' respirators and one known as the 'Mickey Mouse' intended to be less frightening for young children, were also held for issue in an emergency by the wardens. Further equipment; gas rattles, all-clear bells, stirrup pumps and the like were also kept at the Warden Post.

The Air Raid Warden's main rôle in those early months before the outbreak of war, was to visit all the houses in his or her area and measure everyone for respirator size: small, medium, large, or 'Mickey Mouse'. Actual distribution started in September 1938, but there was a delay with the issue of the babies' helmet type respirator, some families having an 'unprotected' infant until the beginning of the war.

Though memorable at the time, most details of A.R.P. service and equipment are now forgotten and there are glaring inaccuracies in films intended to give an impression of war-time England.

5   Social

To many, the most noble of motives for collecting is the recording of social history.

Psychological reasons behind collecting is not an aim of this book; its terms of reference being to suggest what will or could be collected with tomorrow, or the day after, in mind. However, a quick look at the workings of a collector's mind cannot be avoided.

In the late 1970s it is fashionable to label many collecting activities as nostalgia, or, to put it in its clearest terms, a loving look back at some pleasant memory—natural to most people, collectors and non-collectors alike.

Related to collecting, nostalgia is an unfortunate word, implying that we, the collectors of this world, are concerned only with things of the past. It is not only unfortunate but downright harmful if it encourages some collectors to think mainly of yesterday or yesteryear. History did not change into the present some time ago, but at the moment this word is read—not, as far as the reader is concerned, as it is written.

The simple truth is that if a product exists in sufficient variation, then someone, somewhere, will build up a collection. Why? Who cares? It may be that a collection gives a sense of security or timelessness. Perhaps we are inadequate without this prop; the fact remains that some people collect and others do not. If we feel the need to collect, it seems pointless to fight it, but it does seem a good idea to give the desire some positive expression. Collecting items of social significance is one and, as already mentioned, possibly the most noble of such expressions.

Promotional Gifts and Offers

The breakfast cereal was an emerging phenomenon of the 1890s. It all started when, in 1893, an American lawyer by the name of Henry D. Perky started to produce Shredded Wheat. For years he had suffered from dyspepsia and had found relief in boiled wheat

Cadbury's advertising poster, 1905.

and milk for breakfast. At first the product was sold only locally but, in 1895, Perky founded the Natural Food Company at Worcester, Mass., to manufacture Shredded Wheat.

In that same year, 1895, Dr John Kellogg of the Battle Creek Sanitorium, Michigan, began to market Granose Flakes. This was followed in 1898 by Corn Flakes made by the Sanitas Food Company of Battle Creek founded by John's brother William (Kellogg's Corn Flakes were not introduced to Britain until 1924).

The fashion for breakfast cereal had now been set and a large number of manufacturers entered the field, among them the Force Food Company of Canada, who introduced their product to Britain in 1902.

Those of us who can recall the 1930s will remember a promotional character from Force who was given the somewhat sickly name of Sunny Jim:

High on the fence,
On the fence sits Sunny Jim.
Force is the food,
It's the food that raises him.

So went the jingle on Radio Luxemburg.

Force put out a soft toy: Sunny Jim as a promotional gift—certainly now a collector's item—and a plaster point-of-sale shop figure which is now even rarer.

Also in the 1930s was born a promotional 'system' which may be considered a classic of all time. This was the *Cococubs* launched by Cadbury's to boost sales of their cocoa. It was a brilliant concept based on the philosophy of mother buying more cocoa when pressure was put on by her offspring. The 'system' was woven around a series of about 25 miniature lead animals, dressed in natty clothing. There was one human in the series, a boy called Jonathon. One of these figures was packed with every half-pound tin of cocoa, and two with every one pound tin. There were several versions of each animal with different colour combinations of clothing used to 'up date' the models.

There was a clever 'back up' to the series with a Cococub Club; badges with bars to be attached when a member enrolled further Cococubs, newsletters, a completed cut-out village, and even a race game. For the time, the Cococubs were brilliant publicity and a complete set would be worth quite a lot of money at auctions.

It is not known if there are any surviving collections of

Cococubs, but there certainly should be. Cadbury's themselves have very sparse records of the scheme which was of considerable disappointment when material was being gathered for this book.

A less ambitious competitive scheme was launched by Ovaltine, called the *Ovaltinies*, with weekly programmes on Radio Luxemberg. The company have revived the image in the 1970s for their television advertising.

There is little doubt that there are rich pickings for collectors prepared to go to the trouble of finding promotional toys which were pioneered by the producers of cereals and beverages.

Weekend Colour Magazines

It is hard to guess how many people collect the weekend colour magazines that are issued with the national newspapers. There may well be a very large number. On the other hand it is such easy collecting that, if the paper is bought anyway, it is worth a speculative pile in an otherwise empty cupboard. To be in the big league of course, anyone living in Britain would have had to start on 4 February 1962, when the first of *The Sunday Times Colour Section* issues was made.

These weekly releases of potted culture certainly have their place in modern social history and future generations will undoubtedly look to them for an impression of our time, in the same way as *Picture Post* is considered a reflection of the late 1930s through to the 1950s. Only time will tell if today's magazines will be worth more than a few pence a copy.

Postcards

The field of collectors known as *deltiologists* is that of picture postcards, a late nineteenth century phenomenon that, in 1872, began when J. H. Locher of Zürich published a series of six views of that city. In Britain, the law did not permit the use of anything other than plain postcards until 1894; the first publication in that year being George Stewart's *Views of Edinburgh* and F. T. Corkett's *Scenes of Leicester*. Since then picture postcards have teemed off the presses and their study has become one of the more complex of collecting interests.

It is always surprising to a new collector of old postcards how varying are the prices asked for these cards. Fortunately, there are

Postcards 1976:
1. Political caricature.

2. Light Dragoon officer.

3. The Birmingham National Exhibition Centre.

4. The Queen opens the Centre.

a number of works of reference to help the beginner through the jungle.

Established collectors of postcards specialize and newcomers should follow this example, taking for instance, limited areas or subject matter (transport, costume, street furniture, events or commemorations) as a plan of campaign. New cards should be bought in publishers' sets, particularly those of smaller publishers who are likely to engage in short runs.

Printing on Metal

It is inexplicable that the collecting of crown corks does not have more devotees. They have been with us for a long time, from 1892 in fact, when first made by the Crown Cork and Seal Company of Baltimore. Five years later they were being manufactured in Britain.

Crown corks are colourful, attractive, easy to send through the post, and will almost certainly soon share the popularity that beer mats enjoy. The fact that they are more durable than cardboard beer mats should be an encouragement for collectors looking for a *new* interest.

A collection that numbered 6,000 from ninety-six countries in 1974, is owned by Mr Felice Pace, the Vice President of the Hobbies Society of Malta. It was in that year that news of Mr Pace's interest was given in the *Journal of the Institute of Brewing* and the *Soft Drinks Trade Journal*, both British publications to which he had written to trace other collectors.

It was in 1967 that Mr Pace started his 'exceptional collection', as the Italian Ambassador to Malta, Signor R. Masse-Bernucci, called it when he opened a Hobbies Society exhibition.

The collection was built up by making contact with manufacturers and bottlers throughout the world, the best response coming from companies in Britain, Australia, Germany, Belgium and Holland. Two sets are particularly cherished: a 48-cork set issued at the time of the Canadian Expo '67, each crown depicting one of the pavilions at the fair. The other is of 22 crowns issued by the German Löwenbrow Brewery on the occasion of the 1972 Munich Olympic Games, each pictorially representing one of the sporting items held during the Games.

It is really remarkable that the Crown Cork Company at Southall, Greater London, who make over 70 per cent. of all the crown closures used in the United Kingdom, have Felice Pace on their records as the only collector who has consulted them. Here is certainly a collecting theme that is wide open. If Mr Pace put up his collection, framed and classified as it is, at auction, it would undoubtedly gain a very considerable price.

There is a relationship between the crown cork and the disposable safety razor blade. King Camp Gillette used to work for William Painter who invented and patented the crown cork in 1891. It is said that it was the throw-away philosophy of Painter's crown corks that encouraged Gillette to develop his idea of a once only used razor blade, but more about this subject in another chapter.

From crown corks it is not a tremendous step to another printed metal subject worthy of collectors' attention: jam jar lids—today's equivalent of Victorian pot lids. Like most modern printed metal, a collection of jam jar lids will cost nothing to assemble and is well worth a speculative effort. They take up little space and, after a few have been accumulated, some interesting variations in print design over short periods will be noted; changes of type face, size of lettering, etc. Jar lid collecting need not be confined to jam. There are some interesting paste, dressing and sauce lids to build up other divisions of the collection.

To include vintage pieces of printed metal will cost money; a surprisingly large amount when one considers that they were throw-away containers. Tobacco tins, gramophone needle tins, and tea caddies up to the 1960s can all be found in 'antiques' markets priced from a few pence up to about £5. This is a good indication of what to expect when collecting printed metal for tomorrow.

One of the 'classic' series of tinplate containers are those in which Oxo cubes were sold. The dating of them is a study in itself and there is still work to be done in documenting the types. Basically, the smaller tins are of two patterns: a hinged tin to contain twelve cubes and a tin with a push-on lid to hold six cubes. Oxo, it is believed, started using tins after World War I, though the product dates back to 1899 when first made by Fray Bentos in Uruguay. Dating is usually by the printed design on the lids; the early tins having a cubed design, not unlike that used in marquetry and Tunbridge Ware, in red and black, blending to blue and black at the edges, with the drawn turn-over in gilt. Later, the blue and black edging was lost. The next step was to change the cubed

A sample of the many car badges available to collectors.

design to plain red. The final modification came in 1938 or '39 when the red was applied to the turn-over. Dates of these changes are uncertain as are the number of variations in slogans and other printing on the insides of the lid. Add to this the larger sizes of Oxo tins, again, each with its several variations and it will be seen that there is a considerable study to be done. Is it worth it? Yes, some variations are obviously rarer than others and it is about time some logic was put into the crazy arbitrary price structure that exists in this market.

The Brooke Bond Beef Cube tin, introduced shortly before the outbreak of World War II is another interesting package, though it is believed to have kept its original design throughout its short life.

Tobacco tins are already well collected but the similarly shaped boot polish tins are, up to now, neglected, which is surprising. The rotary opening devices being a good basis for study. Here again the field is wide open to collectors looking for something in which to specialize.

A few years ago there were some raised eyebrows and 'ho hos' when the press latched on to a story that beer and other drink cans were collected and that there was a healthy two way trade of the cans across the Atlantic. It was a surprising revelation to those not involved because these cans were of current production. Not a very logical reaction when we consider philately and the enthusiastic collecting of First Day Issues.

Drink cans, though many of us prefer 'real' draught beer, provide an important record of social habit, even humour, with comic strip cartoons on soft drink cans.

An indication of the appeal of printed metal can be seen in the several makes of reproductions available in the shops. Walking through Liberty's London store, the author saw a range of reproduction tinplate tea caddies on display, and was mildly surprised to note they carried the name of a company whose premises are less than a mile away from his home. This is Dodo Designs Limited who market, apart from printed tinplate, enamelled signs and aprons printed with old advertisements. This type of replica production serves the useful purpose of whetting the appetite for the genuine vintage material; items, for example, such as the classic Victory-V sweet tin that incorporated a real clock. One of these spent a long working life on the mantelpiece of the author's grandmother until one of Hitler's bombs ended its career in 1941.

68

Tinplate shoehorns are likely to become popular collectables and a number of dating and identification enquiries have appeared in the press. One interesting example was a shoehorn bearing the name and trademark of the Public Benefit Boot Company, probably made between c.1878 and c. 1886. The trademark of this company, an illustrious name in the boot and shoe trade for many years, was a horse-drawn carriage in the shape of a boot. The shoehorn carried the legend 'Made in Saxony'.

Another German-made shoehorn that has had recent publicity was issued in 1902 at the time of Edward VII's Coronation and carries, apart from the commemorative wording, the advertisement 'Preserve Your Boots by Using The Patent "Hinged Tree". Sold by Buckingham & Son, Boot Makers, Chelmsford.'

The printed metal collecting theme has expanded enormously in the past very few years and will undoubtedly grow stronger as 'real' packaging materials are replaced by synthetics. Some current containers are fine examples of the litho printer's skill and well deserve to be preserved. When Charles Adams patented the process on 13 September 1853, he could not have foreseen how, within 130 years, the products resulting from the process which, after all, was intended as a convenient and low-priced packaging method, would become sought after collectors' items.

Posters and Signs

Posters are not the most satisfactory subject for collecting. They are difficult to display without deterioration and if they are kept rolled and stored it is rather like hiding your light under a bushel. Display of any real number needs considerable wall space, more than most people have available. However, collecting and dealing in posters can be profitable, particularly if the collection is specialized either in period or subject: World Wars I and II, Cinema, Food, Tobacco, Exhibitions, Sporting Events, &c. There is a good market in selling or hiring to film and television companies.

More satisfying but involving greater outlay of cash is the collecting of metal signs. As this is written, a countrywide travelling exhibition is being prepared by two Newcastle-upon-Tyne enthusiasts which will undoubtedly make the subject even more popular than it was hitherto, with a resulting rise in prices.

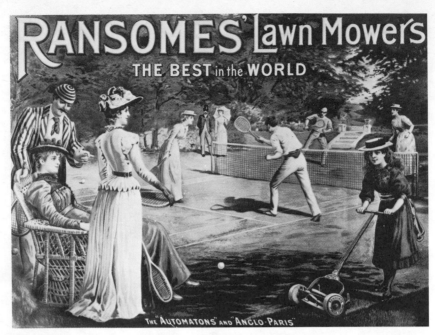

Ransomes advertising poster, early 1900s.

Much work needs to be done researching the makers of metal signs and dating the product advertising. There have been a very great many produced since the mid-nineteenth century, involving enamel, tinplate and embossing. It is hoped that someone will compile a directory of metal sign makers. There is certainly a book to be written.

Further Collecting Suggestions:
    Adhesive Stickers and Transfers
    Admission and Attendance Badges
    Aerosols
    Car Badges
    Chemical Fertilizer and Insecticide Packaging
    Clothes Pegs
    Community Newspapers
    Drug and Patent Medicine Packaging
    Election Literature
    Estate Agents' Handouts
    Health Food Packaging

Holiday Leaflets and Guides
Motor Sales Literature
Pet Food Packaging
Religious Literature
School Textbooks

6   Commercial Reflections

There is no greater constantly changing scene than that of the High
Street, its shops and the goods stocked therein. Marketing
methods, promotional schemes and ad. men, as well as changing
public demand, all contribute to a massive scope for collectors.

Coin-Operated Machines

'Honesty Boxes' were in use in English taverns in the early
seventeenth century. These were tobacco boxes into which a coin
was inserted and a fill of tobacco could be taken out, the amount
being entrusted to the purchaser. They were still in use in the
nineteenth century.

Carl Ade patented an automatic vending machine in Germany in
1867, intended for selling handkerchiefs, cigarettes and sweets.

In 1883, Percival Everitt set up on the platform of London's
Mansion House Underground Station a machine to sell postcards,
and in 1887 the Sweetmeat Automatic Delivery Company was
formed to exploit Everitt's machines, which by that time were
dispensing cigarettes, eggs, quinine, biscuits, scent, handkerchiefs, condensed milk, towels, cough lozenges, sugar, and even
accident insurance.

In France, the Society for the Blind installed machines on
railway stations from 1889.

A British collector of coin-operated vending machines should
make efforts to acquire one of the old Wrigley's Chewing Gum
dispensers, if only because of its social significance. Chewing gum
had been introduced to this country in 1894, as Beeman's Pepsin
Chewing Gum, but it failed to catch the public imagination.
Consequently, the idea of chewing gum died in Britain until it was
reintroduced by Wrigleys in 1911. Then, as earlier, the sweet
shops refused to stock it but, with determination, the manufacturers marketed their product through coin-operated dispensers.

American collectors can go back further and seek the machines of the Adams Gum Company, the first of which were dispensing Tutti-Frutti Gum on the stations of the elevated railroad, New York, in 1888.

If ticket vending machines are to the collector's taste, the interest can go back as far as 1886, when the first in England was invented by James Langley to be installed at the Leamington Athletic Ground, Leeds. But it is unlikely that a collector would be fortunate enough now to find an example of any coin-operated machine from that time. Most have been scrapped and those that have survived command extremely high prices.

Post Office stamp vending machines, introduced in 1891, are particularly sought after, as are the great cast-iron letter boxes.

A real dream for a vending machine collector would be one of the earliest coffee machines. In 1891, one was installed at the Palace of Industry, Paris and, eight years later, two were erected in London: one in Leicester Square and the other in Queens Buildings, Southwark, both by a company with the glorious name of The Pluto Hot Water Syndicate.

The Mills Novelty Company of Chicago whose coin-in-the-slot pin-table bagatelle machines sometimes come to light un-expectedly at auction sales, can claim the credit for helping along the old American habit of peanut eating. It was this company who made the first peanut vending machine for the Pan-American Exposition at Buffalo, N.Y., in 1901.

Since the turn of the century, every conceivable commodity has been packaged for coin-in-the-slot vending.

An out-of-the-run subject in this branch of collecting, examples of which should not be too difficult to acquire, would be parking meters, which first appeared in Britain in 1958. Local authorities scrap and replace their meters from time to time and enquiries at council yards can bring about the purchase of a meter or two as it can lamp posts, bollards and other street furniture, all of which increase in value as they age.

An investment that cannot be recommended for those with a small budget are the relics of the seaside pier; those seemingly ageless, dusty football playing machines, or the Mutascopes— better known as 'What the Butler Saw' machines.

'Modern' amusement and gambling machines would seem a better proposition. They age fairly rapidly and the companies that hire them out very often sell off the replaced models. The weekly

World's Fair is a good source of information about this particular world which was created in 1889 when Charles Frey built the first fruit or 'one-armed-bandit' machine which he christened 'The Liberty Bell'. These were hired out by Frey to San Francisco bars and gambling saloons for 50 per cent. of the profits, making himself a fortune in a very short time.

An interesting related collection is that of gambling machine tokens. Despite some research in this field, the author has yet to discover how many types of these tokens have been produced. It must number several thousand and there does not yet appear to be any serious group of collectors.

In the same year as Frey started hiring his 'Liberty Bell' machines, 1889, an electric operated Edison phonograph with four listening tubes, each with a nickel-in-the-slot mechanism, was installed at the Palais Royal Saloon in San Francisco. The next stage in development was the 'Multiphone' of 1905, made by John C. Dunton of Grand Rapids, Michigan. It stood 7 ft high and enclosed an Edison spring-motor phonograph with a selector mechanism that gave a choice from 24 cylinders.

A year later, 1906, discs were first used on a slot machine called the John Gabel Automatic Entertainer, made by the Automatic Machine and Tool Company, Chicago. The selection was from twenty-four 10 in. diameter discs.

Other early juke-box makers were the Automatic Musical Instrument Company, Grand Rapids, Michigan (1910), and the Seeburg Company, Chicago (1927), but it was not until after the Depression in the early 1930s that mass-production started.

In Britain, the Ditchburn Equipment Company, Lytham St Anne's, Lancashire, first made an all-electric juke-box in 1947.

Coin-operated gas and electric meters came into this branch of collecting and there are more than a few enthusiasts who find meters of all kinds to have veteran appeal. For the earliest coin-operated meters it is possible to go back to 1892 when one hundred meters were fitted for some London customers as an experiment by the South Metropolitan Gas Company.

Cash Registers

It was not many years ago when the highly decorative brass and nickel-plated cash registers of pre-1930s vintage had the hammer put through them in scrap yards. Nobody would think of doing that now; many are used as centre-pieces for antiques shop display and interior decorators, those working on 'Victorian restoration' of pubs, fall over themselves in efforts to buy up what survives.

However, later models of cash registers can still be picked up for the proverbial song. While this book was being written, the author had one given to him by the landlord of a pub. It was a 1930s model and it well represented its period; it was considered too old for conversion when the change over to decimalization coinage was made, and was going to be scrapped.

The collecting of 1930s, '40s and '50s cash registers is strongly recommended for anyone looking for low-cost investment.

The story of the cash register, as distinct from the cash drawer, stems from the summer of 1878 when James Ritty, a restaurant and bar owner of Dayton, Ohio, was on board a liner bound for a trip to Europe. On the voyage he saw a tachometer, the instrument used for counting the revolutions of the propeller shaft. It started him

N.C.R. till, *c.* 1900.

thinking that here could be the basis for a device on which separate bar sales could be recorded.

On returning home, Ritty, with his brother John, a mechanic, began work on such a machine and within a year the first model had been completed. It had two rows of keys across the lower front and a large clock-like dial containing two rows of figures. The hands, controlled by keys, indicated dollars and cents on the dial. This

Cash registers: two of the very earliest, and models from the 1930s and 1950s.

prototype had two adding discs that totalled the sales made during the day, but there was no cash drawer.

In the same year, 1879, two further models were built at Dayton, one having the 'tablet' form of indication, with other improvements. This was called 'Ritty's Incorruptible Cashire'. There are no records of these models being offered for sale.

The next model was known as the 'Paper Roll Machine', and was the first cash register to be marketed. Instead of adding discs, it had a wide paper roll inside the cabinet, mounted horizontally above and across the keyboard. Each key operated a pin that pierced a hole in the appropriate column of the paper roll. If, for instance, there were ten holes in the 5-cent column at the time of balancing, it showed that 50-cents of business had been transacted in 5-cent sales.

John H. Patterson, the proprietor of a miners' supply store, was a worried man. His store should have been showing a profit of $12,000 per year but, instead, it was losing $3,000 and he was in debt to the extent of $16,000 after a three year period of trading. On investigation he found that some assistants had been undercharging customers for their own gain. After sacking the culprits he telegraphed Dayton for 'two of those machines that register sales' without even enquiring the price.

Within six months of the arrival of the machines, Patterson's store debts were reduced to $3,000 and the books showed a profit.

Patterson was later to buy the controlling interest in the National Manufacturing Company that had been formed by Ritty.

Selling the cash register was not easy and to overcome opposition from antagonistic shop assistants, all the company's salesmen were equipped with miniature three-key cash registers— these are now highly prized collectors' items. Carried in a small case, one of these miniatures could be demonstrated to the shop proprietor in a back room, after which the salesman could leave through the shop unmolested.

One of the attachments that has disappeared from the more modern cash registers is the 'argument settler', a glass-sided contraption fixed to the side of the body of the machine. The amount was rung up and, instead of being placed in the drawer, the coin was put in a slot at the top of the attachment. So, if the customer claimed he had tendered a larger value coin than he had been given change for, the shopkeeper or bartender could prove his point by showing the coin through the glass.

Advertising Ashtrays and Water Jugs

To suggest the collecting of advertising ashtrays and water jugs is to invite rebuke for encouraging pilferage from pubs. But it is possible to build up a collection without resorting to dishonesty. Jugs and ashtrays frequently turn up in junk shops and many pub landlords will accommodatingly support a local collection. This theme is a logical step up from beer mats and has the added attraction of being concerned with ceramics, a traditional collectors' interest.

Jugs and ashtrays have been and are produced for breweries and distillers by a number of notable potteries: Doulton, Wade, and Hancock, Corfield & Waller Limited. In passing, a dating point about the latter named company may be of use to some tyro collectors. The foundation date was 1891 when the style was Hancock & Corfield Limited. Products were thus marked until 1918 when the name was changed to that still in current use.

Advertising Calendars

A certain New York insurance company could not have known what they had started when they produced the world's first advertising calendar in 1845.

It is impossible to know how many million calendars bearing publicity material have been published since this or, for that matter, how many appear each year. Rising production costs have somewhat reduced the numbers and some of us who are not directly concerned with commercial enterprise often have to beg calendars and diaries from others, or are even forced to buy one!

Collectors of calendars are faced with a problem of selection. There are, of course, the obvious choices such as the Pirelli avant garde photographic calendar which, although no longer produced, is sought after throughout the world as an office prestige symbol as well as a collectors' item, and the Schweppes Racing Calendar, both of which have established for themselves a place in advertising history.

The Pirelli series of calendars began in 1964, the work of the Beatles photographer Robert Freeman, working with art director Derek Forsyth and designer Derek Birdsall on location in Majorca. The quantity produced of this first calendar was 35,000.

Subsequent Pirelli calendars were as follows:

1965
Photographer: Duffy.   Designer: Colin Forbes.
Location: South of France.   Number of copies: 36,000

1966
Probably the first British calendar to be the subject of its own press conference.
Photographer: Peter Knapp.   Designer: Colin Forbes.
Location: Club Méditerranée, Al Hoceima, Morocco.
Number of copies: 36,000.

1967
There was no Pirelli calendar for this year as it was felt there was a risk of the idea becoming stale.

1968
The calendar returned with a new format.
Photographer: Harri Peccinotti.   Designer: Derek Birdsall.
Ancient and modern poems illustrated photographically.
Number of copies: 40,000

1969
Photographer: Harri Peccinotti. Designer: Derek Birdsall.
Location: Big Sur, California, with local girls as models.
Number of copies: 60,000

1970
Photographer: Francis Giacobetti.
Location: Paradise Island in the Bahamas.
Number of copies: 43,000

1971
Photographer: Francis Giacobetti.
Location: a private beach near Montego Bay, Jamaica.
Number of copies: 43,000

1972
Photographer: Sarah Moon.
Location: a decaying mansion in the Malmaison area of Paris.
Number of copies: 45,000.

1973
Winner for Pirelli Limited of the Design and Art Designers' Association best British calendar award.

Artist: Allen Junes.
All work—a fusion of art and photography—carried out in Britain.
Number of copies: 43,000.

1974
Tenth anniversary production.
Photographer: Hans Feurer.
Location: Seychelles.

Pirelli Limited announced retirement from calendar publishing in March 1974, with the explanation that it was '. . . felt we should withdraw while still, as some commentators have been kind enough to remark, at the top.'

Labelled the 'world's greatest office status symbol' and the 'Rolls Royce of calendars', a flourishing 'black market' developed, the highest known price fetched by an individual copy being £60.

Slightly down the scale are the calendars of Guinness and Whitbread, both highly desirable acquisitions for collectors.

As in most fields of collecting, it is essential to specialize in the publicity of a small number of companies, adding annually to each series.

One type of calendar to be avoided is the *syndicated* product, when a publisher uses a similar design for a number of companies. These are usually of the 'girlie' type and carry the names of smaller local bookmakers and car hire companies. The production runs of these are long and the quality often poor.

Bank Cheques

A difficult but rewarding theme for a collection is bank cheques. Difficult because they are not the sort of thing that people want to let out of their possession. For that reason they have a quality of rareness and therefore a collection could be well worth establishing.

It is possible to go back at least to 1763 for printed cheques. The oldest surviving example being of that date, issued by Hoare's Bank.

Probably the best way to collect is to let it be known in one's circle of friends that a collection is being started and blank (unsigned) or cancelled cheques would be appreciated. Good friends may even be encouraged to go through long forgotten papers in desk drawers to rake out some real old fine vintage pieces!

Branded cigarettes started in Britain about the year 1859 and were made by Robert Peacock Gloag in Deptford Lane, London, under the name Sweet Threes. Cigarettes had been produced before this date but did not carry a brand name.

Sweet Threes were made from Latakia dust rolled in yellow tissue paper and were fitted with cane mouth pieces. They were sold in bundles of ten for six pence ($2\frac{1}{2}$ p).

Like many of the brands that followed, Sweet Threes have long been extinct, but there are some surviving names from the nineteenth century: Passing Clouds (introduced 1874), Gold Flake (1883), Woodbines (1888), Player's Navy Cut (1892) and Three Castles (1878). The latter brand was the first to be sold in cardboard packets (from 1892) while others—except Weights which were sold by weight unwrapped—were sold in paper wrappers which were easily crushed. Some makers put in cardboard stiffeners in the paper wrappers, a trend that started with another Wills' brand, Globe, in the early 1880s. It was this practice that gave rise to cigarette cards, the stiffeners being printed with pictures that could be collected.

Like confectionery wrappers, the design of cigarette packets reflect fashion changes in graphic design and advertising art and the subject is well worth the attention of collectors.

More appealing to some, but still in the same field, is collecting tobacco tins. In recent years quite a cult has been woven round printed tin boxes and hardly a day passes without an enquiry being received by the author about the origin of some extinct brand of tobacco. It is another of those fields of research that needs to be more deeply explored. Tobacco trade journals are useful for consultation when seeking active dates of specific brands but often, in common with other commodities such as the lesser known brands of soap and polishes of all kinds, identification and dating can be very difficult.

The shape and style of manufacture of metal containers can be a useful guide: the way the seams are made or if the body of the tin is 'deep drawn'; the type of closure seal; ventilation holes (if any); method of forming the hinge; and whether or not it has rolled-over edges; these are all pointers to the date of manufacture. It is a specialized subject that would take up too much space if dealt with here. It is known that at least one book covering this kind of

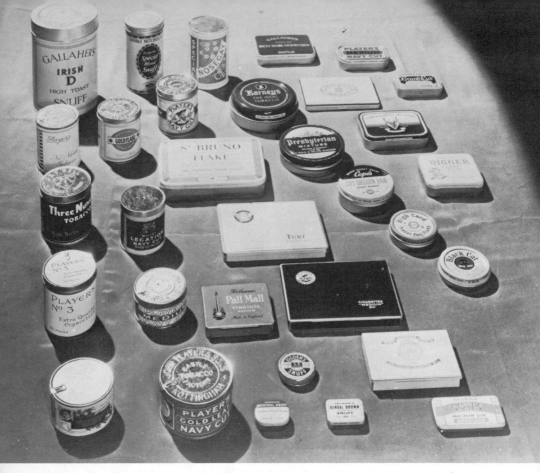

A medley of tobacco and snuff tins, hinged and prise-off lids.

information is in the course of preparation, and its publication will add enormously to our store of product history.

But let us not despise the modern tobacco tin. It is a disappearing artefact—being replaced by the pouch-type plastic and paper container. Tins being made now will surely be sought after in ten years time.

There is some interesting point-of-sale publicity material connected with tobacco. A pre-World War II tobacconist counter sale dispenser was of iron. They were often of similar pattern carrying different raised lettering: 'Players 6d.', 'Capstan 6d', 'Players 1/-', etc., relics of the days when prices were not subjected to continual and frequent increases.

82

Potato Crisp Bags

Those who like *real junk*; disposables that cost nothing to collect and which will build up into a picture of the changing social tastes of our time, are recommended to consider the enormous variety of potato crisp packaging that is available. It is exactly the type of thing that tomorrow's collectors of ephemera will be seeking.

Although produced by a large number of small firms in nineteenth century America, potato crisps came late to Britain, one of the pioneers being Carter's Crisps of London, which started production in 1913. One of the company's employees was one Frank Smith who, in 1920, left the firm to start his own manufacturing concern. In a few years he was in a position to take over Carter's.

Confectionery Wrappers

Chocolate Box Art—the derogatory term used to describe the mass-produced pop visual, stems from 1868, when Cadbury's used a picture of a wistful looking girl child holding a kitten. This was used on boxes for chocolate dragées.

Chocolate boxes are collected, both the pictorial examples and purely lettered boxes. The latter are, one feels, more representative of the period in which they were made as lettering styles do so perfectly reflect contemporary fashion and taste.

From chocolate boxes it is but a brief step to the chocolate bar wrapper and sweet packets. Packets which look 'old fashioned', Callard and Bowser Butterscotch, have undergone subtle changes in design over the years and a collection of this make alone would make a fascinating collection. Likewise, the wrappers of chocolate bars can be interesting. The long-dead Double Six, Five Boys, and Caramello bars would bring back fond memories to many, and a selection of the wrappers seen on the counters of sweet shops today are guaranteed to inspire nostalgia in a few years time.

The Cadbury's Dairy Milk Chocolate label-wrapper has undergone a number of changes since its introduction in 1902 when it was light blue, the colour being changed to the now familiar dark blue in 1915. The really radical and regrettable change came in 1951 when Cadbury's dropped the 'CDM' milking bucket from the design in favour of a 'neater' styling.

DEVELOPMENT IN DAIRY MILK LABEL DESIGN

1907

1935

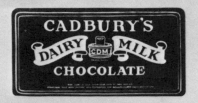

1915

1940

1923

1951

1933

1961

Design and Cadbury's Dairy Milk wrappers.

When the author was running a stall in a London antiques market he was asked one day by a customer if there were any old toffee wrappers in stock. Thinking that this was perhaps a critical reflection on the goods on display, a somewhat guarded reply was given. It was only when conversation turned to the printing differences between 1927 and 1928 Dainty Dianas that it was realised that here was a serious enquiry. So there it is; some collectors are already going in for this form of ephemera.

Slogans and Logos

The advertising slogan is so much a part of life that it is easy to forget that nowadays many slogans are short lived. A contrast to Britain's first advertising slogan in regular use was: 'Beecham's Pills "Worth a Guinea a Box"', which was introduced in 1849 and was carried on until World War II.

There is certainly need for specialist records of slogans and here is scope for individual collectors.

The same applies to logos, as opposed to trademarks which are officially recorded since 1876, when the trademark of Bass's Pale Ale was registered. Logos are born, change and die without trace, and before many years have passed there will be expressions of regret that no library of logos was established when they were blossoming all over the commercial field.

A library of this kind, once established, could also record the mass of advertising competitions that have been promoted since Police Plug Tobacco ran the first known such competition in the Pennsylvania press in 1884.

Collecting need not be necessarily confined to tangible objects and can be equally, if not more, rewarding if greater ephemeral aspects are explored.

Trade Ephemera

The signs are that the collecting of trading ephemera: bills, business cards, letter-heads and trade catalogues, the work of jobbing printers, is about to see a very definite revival.

There is no aspect of social history with more constant change than the High Street trading scene, and the appeal of related ephemera is multi-fold: period lettering styles, commodity prices, traders' names and addresses.

Advertisement from Pears soap, *c.* 1894.

The first systematic collector of this class of ephemera seems to have been Ambrose Heal (1872–1959), who wrote authoritative works on London's shopsigns and tradesmen's cards. Another collection, now in the Bodleian Library, was accumulated by Dr John Johnson, Printer to the University of Oxford, who died in 1956.

A collection of grocery bills, dated between 1782 and 1812, in the possession of London bookseller Ben Weinreb, was the subject of an article in *The Times* of 30 July 1977.

Not only old material need be regarded as collectable. Up-to-date items such as printed carrier bags, 'flyers', and the like, are beginning to become sought after. The author can modestly claim to have a little to do with this movement. A couple of suitcases full of paper and plastic carrier bags were taken on the train from Tunbridge Wells to Birmingham to make an appearance on BBC Television's *Pebble Mill at One* programme. Before the programme had ended several calls were received from collectors anxious to swop bags. A number of letters of thanks later arrived from people looking for something original to collect.

Further Collecting Suggestions:
  Advertising Novelties
  Airline and Hotel Consumables
  Bread Wrappers
  Cigar Tubes
  Fruit Wrappers
  Point-of-Sale Publicity
  Seed Packets
  Trade Directories (Yellow Pages)
  Wine Labels
  Yoghurt Tubs

7 Pop, Fashion and Vanity

Those of us old enough to remember the 1950s as if they were only last year will recall how dated, even ugly, seemed the fashions and adornments of twenty years earlier. The author can look with a feeling of tender sadness on an episode in 1951. One of those lamp shades with fabric suspended from an anodized metal ring, a popular design of the late 1920s and early '30s, came to light from under a heap of rubbish in the garage. My mother had a trace of tears in her eyes when she remembered buying it and how *chic* it seemed at the time. Frankly, it looked extremely ugly, though doubtless it would now command a few pounds in the Raz-a-ma-taz breed of shops.

Appreciation is different today and few people condemn or ridicule products of twenty or even ten years back. Quite the contrary, many surround these things with a veneration they scarcely deserve. The remarkable Teddy Boy (or Girl) cult and its complementary Rock and Roll fever, typifying certain aspects of the mid-1950s, has a strong band of adherents though, strangely, the 'spiv' fashion of a few years before is almost entirely neglected. Nostalgia is a strange business! However, it is reasonable to suppose that this trend of looking back to popular images, be they fashion or music, will continue, and the collecting of such paraphernalia of today will be financially rewarding within a comparatively short span of years.

Top of the Pops

A surprising thing to emerge in this throw-away age of *pop* is the virtual disappearance of gramophone records of comparatively recent vintage. For a long time we have been aware of the collectability of 78 r.p.m. records and how rarer examples can command high prices. But now it seems that the more modern 45 r.p.m. singles can, in some cases, be even more valuable. The revival of Rock 'n Roll of the 1950s and the recent death of the king of that style, Elvis Presley, have revealed that some records of which hundreds of thousands of pressings were made, are now virtually non-existent or, where they do survive, their condition is deplorable. This is particularly true of chart records—those of the 'top twenty', most of which are played to death within a few weeks of their purchase or thrown away to make room for the latest releases.

There is certainly a case for investing collectors to keep a mint conditioned library of recordings that are nominated as 'top ten' or, if finances permit, 'top twenty'.

What, one wonders, would be the value of an unplayed collection of the November 1952 Top Ten, the first time such a list was published by the *New Musical Express*. This collection would comprise:

1   *Here is My Heart* Al Martino.
2   *You Belong to My Heart* Jo Stafford.
3   *Somewhere Along the Way* Nat King Cole.
4   *Isle of Innisfree* Bing Crosby.
5   *Feet Up* Guy Mitchell.
6   *Half As Much* Rosemary Clooney.
7   *High Noon* Frankie Laine and
    Forget Me Not Vera Lynn.
8   *Sugar Bush* Doris Day and Frankie Laine, and
    Blue Tango Ray Martino.
9   *Homing Waltz* Vera Lynn.
10 *Auf Wiedersehen* Vera Lynn.

Costume and Fashion

Costume is a well established collecting theme and it is hardly necessary to evangelize the cause in this book. Somewhat less popular is the collecting of examples of materials themselves, especially man-made fibres. There may be a few raised eyebrows at this idea but it must be remembered that synthetics have a venerable history.

It was in 1664 that Dr Hooke, Curator of Experiments to the Royal Society, wrote in *Micrographia* that there might be found a way 'to make an artificial glutinous composition much resembling, if not fully as good as—nay better than—that excrement or whatever substance it be which the silk worm wire draws its claws.' Although the eighteenth century French scientist Réaumur

A printed sweat shirt. Fashion of the 1970s.

considered artificial fibres to be practicable, it was not until the nineteenth century that a patent was taken out by George Andeman, a Swiss chemist, for dissolving and re-precipitating wood pulp and other cellulose materials.

Later in the nineteenth century, both Edison and Swan produced suitable fibres for electric lamp filaments, Joseph Swan patenting in 1883 a method of making fibres by forcing nitro-cellulose in acetic acid through a series of holes.

At the 1889 Paris Exposition the Comte Hilaire de Chardonnet exhibited an artificial silk which he called 'rayon'. A German factory followed this with a product called 'glanzstoff', and soon three English chemists, Cross, Bevan and Beadle, were working on a viscose rayon process.

The first knitted rayon stockings appeared in 1910, made by the German company of Bemberg and, in the 1920s, through the work of Dr Leo Lillienfeld, motor car tyres were made using a high-tenacity viscose rayon.

In 1938, the discovery of Nylon 6.6 was announced by the American Dr Wallace Carothers. It was later to be produced by the Du Pont Corporation.

The chemically different Terelene was discovered in 1941 and, since then, there has been a multitude of man-made fibres: elastomeric (stretchable), acrylic (for fleecy, knitted and tufted fabrics), glass (for upholstery and curtains), metallic (non-tarnishable metal fibres), polyoefin (for cordage and webbing) and polyvinyl chloride (for leather-like products).

Items made from these materials, particularly early examples, make a technically important collection, and one well within the financial scope of most people.

To return to the theme of fashion. The *bikini* two-piece swimming attire typifies the 'liberation' trend of post World War II fashion more than any other item of female dress, and the very name stands as a landmark in the history of mankind. Early examples are surely to achieve high prices in the foreseeable future. It was on 5 July 1946, at a Paris fashion show staged by couturier Louis Reard, that the garment first appeared, modelled by Micheline Bernadi, a dancer. This was four days after an atomic bomb was exploded on the Pacific atoll of Bikini, and Reard used the word to express the ultimate. It is said that the model received 50,000 letters as a result of the publicity given in the world press.

In England in 1950, a young lady was told by the police to get dressed when she attempted to try out a bikini. But the bikini and more, or less, depending on how you looked at it, was here to stay; in some ways like the mini-skirt nearly twenty years later, a sign of female emancipation.

Tea Towels and T-Shirts

As this book was being typed a letter was received from a lady in Didcot whose mother has assembled a collection of over seventy tea towels. And what a good idea it seems!

Perhaps even more reflective of current life is the collecting of T-Shirts. There are some designers who are treating the subject as nothing less than an artform, while other producers have specialized in short runs for pubs and clubs. This has come about in very recent years and who is to say if the trend will last. If it is a fashion of short duration these special runs will certainly be tomorrow's curios.

Contemporary T-shirt designs.

The author must confess to never having seen a collection of clothing fasteners, though the collecting of buttons is a common and popular activity. The collecting writer George Mell was recently telling the author of the progress made in the collecting of 'bachelor buttons'—those metal contrivances that replace missing buttons without the need of sewing. They are also used where detachable buttons are required in the case of frequently cleaned boiler suits and overalls. There have been many patterns and makes of bachelor buttons and it is surprising that no publisher has brought out a specialist book on the subject.

Collectors looking for something unusual could do worse than look to dress fasteners other than buttons; press-stud fasteners for instance, which were first produced by John Newnham in 1860.

The zip so typifies our period of history that we are inclined to dismiss it as a collecting subject. Nevertheless, there is here an intriguing story of invention. The innovation is attributed to Whitcomb L. Judson of Chicago, who intended if for use on boots and shoes. When, in 1893, it was exhibited at the Chicago Exposition, it was taken up by a Colonel Lewis Walker who founded the Automatic Hook and Eye Company to make the fastener at a factory in Meadville, Pennsylvania. The company did not achieve much commercial success. Nor did the Walker's Universal Fastener Company which produced the 'C-Curity', an improved device, from 1902.

More successful was the 'separable fastener' patented by Gideon Sundbach of Hoboken, New Jersey, in April 1913. Colonel Walker purchased the rights of this and marketed it as the Talon Slide Fastener.

There was considerable public mistrust of zip-fasteners, but the sales breakthrough came in 1917 when the American Navy used them for flying clothing, the Army for pocket closures, and the Air Corps for attaching fabric to airframes.

In Britain, the first zip, called the Ready Fastener, was made in Birmingham by Kynoch in 1919, but it was eight years before any British clothing manufacturer fitted zips to products for 'off-the-peg' sales.

Even after World War II the zip fastener was not universal and as late as the mid-1950's trousers were closed by buttons.

Eye glasses are ancient in origin, with written evidence dating from 1289. There have been a number of important landmarks since then: spectacles with side pieces, known as temple spectacles, were introduced by Edward Scarlett in 1727; bi-focal lenses were invented by Benjamin Franklin and described by him in a letter of 23 March 1785; tinted window glass was used for sunglasses in 1885; contact lenses were devised in 1887 by Dr A. Eugen Frick of Zürich and manufactured by Zeiss of Jena.

There is a nice comment on spectacles and fashion to be found in *The Optician and Photographic Trades Review* of 12 January 1893:

'A female interviewer on the staff of a well-known woman's paper has been interviewing a West-end optician. The gentleman complained bitterly that his trade had been so seriously injured by the 'insensate' decree of fashion that 'mashers' should no longer wear eye glasses. The loss has, however, been compensated for in some degree, for we frequently see women who move in the 'big life' adorned [?] with monocles, and there is still the more prevailing fashion of wearing lorgnettes. This latter contrivance is certainly artistic, if not always useful—we mean to those ladies who use them solely to add to their charms. The optician to whom we have referred naively told the interviewer that "among those who wish to adopt glasses for appearance there are defects in vision which I do my best to remedy, but in the greater majority a perfectly clear pebble proves satisfactory." '

Today, Victorian spectacle frames command high prices in antiques shops and collectors with tomorrow in mind would be better advised to consider more modern spectacles for investment collecting. By careful buying from junk shops it is still possible to build up a representative collection of fashion frames from the 1920s, '30s, '40s and '50s for a few pounds. Most homes have a few unwanted pairs of spectacles and, once the interest becomes known among friends, donated frames are more than likely to be forthcoming.

Cosmetic Containers

There is nothing really new about collecting cosmetic containers. The making of perfume bottles has been a respectable artform for many years but collecting has been restricted to a comparatively small hard core. Possibly the greatest name in the art of production

Group portrait: cosmetic containers.

glass making was René Lalique. Born at Ay (Marne), France, on 6 April 1860, his early profession was that of a jeweller and, towards the end of the last century, was making his considerable mark— Lalique brooches and combs in *art nouveau* 'Liberty' style were shown at the Paris International Exhibition of 1900, where they attracted great attention and acclaim.

It was in 1908 that Lalique opened his glass works in Paris, at first to make perfume bottles and all manner of decorative and functional items, from electric light fittings to fruit bowls and, of course, car mascots, for which, if anything, he is even better known than as a maker of perfume bottles.

Lalique's glass was formed in plaster moulds, using mass-production methods, but the hand-finishing was to the highest standards. The products of the factory were characterized by 'iced' surfaces, elaborated patterns and/or colour in relief.

Lalique perfume bottles command high prices, as do all the factory's products when they come up at auction. Even so, they are an excellent investment.

The collector should not despise perfume bottles of lesser repute. They are, almost without exception, attractive works of industrial art and worthy of considerably more recognition than they generally receive.

Some of the 'outer' packaging of perfume can also be fun to collect. There was the classic, slightly *risqué*, blue Bakelite outer of the 'Evening in Paris' perfume depicting a hotel bedroom door with two pairs of shoes outside. You were considered quite a 'card' to give your girlfriend this as a present in the 1930s.

Lipstick containers can be very satisfying things to collect, particularly as one can usually get them for nothing. When acquaintances know that they are being collected, they often are very willing to donate used or unwanted lipsticks. Fortunate collectors may even find the original metal cartridge lipsticks that were first marketed in the U.S.A. by Maurice Levy in 1915. Since then there has been a multitude of lipstick cartridges manufactured all over the world, many using plastic materials in a highly artistic and pleasing way.

In the 1977 centenary booklet, *100 Years of Shopping at Boots*, our attention is drawn to Boots' own brand cosmetic jars that appeared early in this century, such as Boots' Cherry Tooth Paste and Boots' Face Cream, which fetch up to £5 each. To quote from the booklet, 'It is interesting to speculate whether today's cosmetics from the Boots' No 7 or No 17 ranges will become antiques fifty years from now'.

The answer is 'no', they will not be *antiques* in fifty years time—wrong term—but they certainly will be collectable.

Further Collecting Suggestions:
  Clothing Labels
  Knitting and Dressmaking Patterns
  Neckties and Belts

8   Mechanical

It was the maturing of the veteran and vintage movement in motoring that laid the foundation for the collecting of small machinery of the past. When the film *Genevieve*, starring a 1904 Darracq in the title rôle, was made in the 1950s, venerable vehicles were the subject of the derogatory term 'Old Crocks'—an expression seldom heard today. Of course, Lord Montagu, with his founding and nurturing of what is now the National Motor Museum, did much to giving the interest in mechanical collecting an air of acceptance. Now, it goes without saying that any well kept car of more than fifteen years of age will turn a few heads in the High Street.

So it goes down the line to sewing machines and typewriters—the typescript of this book, by the way, is being worked on a 1906 Remington No 10—but respect for these smaller machines is quite new. Very few years back sewing machines such as Willcox & Gibbs of the last century could be picked up at auctions for less than £1. In 1978 they sell for around £28, which is not a bad investment increase over 5 or 6 years.

The indications are that prices will continue to rise as more people take an active interest in mechanical relics and, in the opinion of the author, this is one of the most rewarding and pleasurable branches of collecting.

One can do worse than accumulate a number of mechanical items which are well collected: sewing machines, typewriters, cash registers, mangles, etc. But there are other machines worthy of the attention of a collector with an eye to profit.

Television and Radio Receivers

Early in 1976, a researcher of one of the companies of Independent Television called the author on the telephone to ask if he knew the whereabouts of some 1955 television receivers, for a programme to celebrate the 21st anniversary of the opening of commercial

Marconiphone 3-valve receiver, 1923.

television in Britain. This was a challenge to be taken up and, though numerous calls to manufacturers and old established dealers proved fruitless, fifteen suitably dated sets were eventually acquired in time for the programme. A paragraph in the local newspaper led to their discovery in attics and garages—many were still in working condition. Not only were the receivers found but also the appendages of the period: convertor units that enabled existing sets to screen the second channel, and magnifying lenses which were clipped to the fronts of sets to make the picture seem larger—in 1955 screens were still generally small.

The fact that a large television company had to enlist outside help to find industrially produced articles which were in use only 21 years earlier, illustrates how quickly mass-manufactured products can become hard-to-find, and even rare.

A real prize in this field would be the discovery of any of the television receivers produced in the early 1930s; The Baird Mirror Drum Televisor of 1933 by Bush Radio Limited, The Griffin of 1933 by Griffin Radio Limited, any model by Plew Television Limited, a *Daily Express* sponsored construction kit of 1934 by Mervyn Sound & Vision Limited, a 1935 set by Gillavision Television, or the lowest priced set of 1935 which was built by Bennett Television for sale at £3 5 shillings (£3.25).

The fact that early radio equipment is acknowledged as a collecting subject was born from the enthusiasm with which visitors viewed an exhibition at the Victoria & Albert Museum late in 1977, presented by the British Vintage Wireless Society. There is no need to persuade enthusiasts that early wireless makes a valuable and important collection. On the other hand, modern examples of miniaturized radio technology are sadly neglected and it is doubtful if a comprehensive exhibition of radios for the period 1955–77 could be staged. There could be a worse decision than to specialize in current and recently out-of-production transistorized receivers.

Recorders

Collecting of early phonographs and gramophones for both investment and interest has gained such popularity in recent years and prices have reached such heights that it is reasonable to believe that values have started to level off. That is not to say that the bottom will fall out of the market but there are other, even allied subjects to collect that will probably increase in value at a greater rate. One of these subjects is likely to be wire and tape recorders.

Although recorders were made for broadcasting and film use from as early as 1929, it was in 1947 that the industry really began, when the Brush Development Company, Cleveland, Ohio, produced the Soundmirror for home use.

Hearing Aids

To justify the collecting of hearing aids to a sceptic one must appeal to latent admiration of invention. There has been an enormous development in this field from the simple ear trumpet to the super-miniaturized, almost undetectable appliances of the present time. A collection covering hearing aids over the past 80 years could readily pay for itself quickly in hire fees for shop window displays.

The first electric hearing aid was the Acousticon, patented by Miller Reese Hutchinson of New York in November 1901. Hutchinson was also the inventor of the Klaxon horn—so he had both ends of the market! The Acousticon, a large instrument with a telephone type receiver and heavy batteries, was put in production in 1902 by the newly formed Hutchinson Acoustic Company.

One of the first users of an electric hearing aid was Queen Alexandra who had one available for the coronation ceremony in 1902. Its American inventor, Victor Ketjet, was given a medal as a mark of appreciation. This instrument was stolen early in 1977 from a shop vault in Arnhem, Holland.

Early electric hearing aids used heavy batteries that had to be carried. It was not until 1935, when the Amplivox, marketed by A. Edwin Stevens of London, was introduced, that batteries were small enough to be worn, clipped to a pocket. Further miniaturization followed with the introduction of the transistorized hearing aid in December 1952, by the Sonotone Corporation of Elmsford, New York.

Cycles

There is nothing new about collecting cycles. There has been a hardcore of enthusiasts assembling collections of these faithful

Raleigh 'Strika' bicycle, 1977.

Bickerton folding bicycle, 1977.

machines for years, and antiques shops are not reluctant to display a penny farthing (more correctly called an 'Ordinary'). What has been neglected by collectors with an eye to the future is the auxiliary engined bicycle; the forerunners of the mopeds and scooters. The collection could comprise the motors with or without the cycles themselves. The subject is ideal for anyone with a mechanical turn of mind; a collector who would dearly like to be involved in veteran, vintage or classic motor vehicle activities but, through lack of cash or space, is unable to do so.

Fire Extinguishers

This is a somewhat neglected theme, which is surprising when it is realised that antique examples are aesthetically pleasing as well as being examples of inventive skill.

The earliest extinguishers were glass balls filled with a saline solution, designed for throwing into the heart of the fire, dating back to 1734 when invented by a German physician by the name of Fuches. This type continued to be made until World War I.

Compressed air cylinder extinguishers that could be squirted

An example of the commonplace photograph becoming an historic record; one of the first Bowser automatic petrol pumps installed in a Manchester garage in 1921.

into a fire were invented by George William Manby in 1816, and were made by Hadley, Simkin and Lott, Long Acre, London. Such a find would be prized by a collector as this company's production was soon discontinued. This form of fire fighting equipment was revived in the 1860s by several manufacturers.

The smaller CTC (carbon tetrachloride) extinguishers are the most convenient to collect and there is sufficient variety to make an attractive collection.

The Brighouse, Yorkshire, company of J. Blakeborough & Sons Limited made valves from 1828. In 1926 they entered the fire extinguisher market with the Nu-Swift pressure-charge-operated Model 1000. The 2-gallon Nu-Swift Universal Water/Co2 extinguisher followed in 1935, and a 2-gallon Air Foam upright model in 1946. The later extinguisher trend, the Dry Powder type, was introduced by Nu-Swift in 1957. All these 'innovation' models by this company will be highly collectable when it is generally realised that fire extinguishers are worthy of specialization.

Lawn Mowers

There is one machine which is sadly neglected as a collectable item; the lawn mower. This is regrettable as they do have great charm and the veteran examples are gems of cast iron. The three veteran and vintage machines of the author (very much a non-gardening enthusiast) are in use regularly during the summer months and great pleasure they give! The stable comprises a 1906 Ransome Automaton, a Green's Silens Messor of the same period and a 1928 Atco motor mower. After some years of using machines of this kind it is hard to understand why the suburban gardeners at weekends are not competing with each other for the best conditioned venerable machine in the neighbourhood. Fashion has not yet gone that far—it stops at cars, typewriters and sewing machines.

This message may bring in some converts, so a somewhat more extensive history might be appropriate.

The mowing machine was the invention, in 1830, of Edwin Beard Budding of Stroud, Gloucestershire, who, as a youth, worked in the Brimscombe Mills which was owned by a family called Lewis. John Lewis had developed a rotary cutting machine for clipping the nap from cloth; a machine made by James Ferrabee & Company at the Phoenix Ironworks in Stroud. It is said that Budding had the idea of his grass mower while watching the nap cutter in action.

The first lawn mowers were produced in the factory of James Ferrabee in 1830. The cutting width was 19 ins and the machine was pushed from the rear, but a second handle was provided at the front so that when cutting on difficult ground the mower could be pushed and pulled simultaneously. At the rear was a roller which, by means of gears, drove a cylinder comprising the cutting blades. The cylinder was geared to rotate at about twelve times that of the rear roller. The cutting action was by means of the blades of the cylinder working against a rigid knife bar on the underside of the machine, thus providing a scissor action.

As is the case of many important inventions, the lawn mower did not receive immediate enthusiasm and Edwin Budding died in 1848, at the age of 50, never knowing the popularity his brainchild would receive.

By 1833, lawn mowers were selling under the name of Ransomes, and Ferrabee modified the original conception and continued marketing under their name.

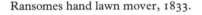

Ransomes hand lawn mover, 1833.

Alexander Shanks Junior, of Arbroath, registered the design of a 'grass cutting and rolling machine' in July 1842. This machine had a width of 42 ins!

Shortly after the introduction of the Shanks machine, the Leeds company of Thomas Green & Son entered the market. Ferrabee abandoned production, leaving Ransomes, Shanks and Green as the 'big three', a situation that lasted for the following 120 years.

Picksley Sims of Leigh produced a range of mowers in 1859, closely followed by Barnard, Bishop and Barnard of Norwich, who made The Patent Noiseless Lawn Mower.

In the U.S.A. probably the first maker of lawn mowers was the Coldwell Lawn Mower Company, founded by English born Thomas Coldwell.

Fellows and Bates Limited entered the market with a side-wheel machine and claimed, in 1871, to have sold 5,000 of these machines during that year. Greens claimed the sale of 6,000 Silens Messor machines.

Other nineteenth century makers included B. Hirst & Sons, Halifax, who made the Patent Self Adjusting Lawn Mower from

Ransomes motor mower, 1903.

1867; W. H. Boulton & Company (later Boulton & Paul), Norwich, makers of the Eclipse mower from 1872; Hartley & Sugden Limited, Halifax, makers of Victoria and Windsor machines from 1874; John Crowley & Company, Manchester and Sheffield, makers of the Invincible machine from 1874; Barford & Perkins, Peterborough, makers of Godiva and Beatrice from 1886; and E. H. Benthall & Company Limited, Malden, makers of the Patent Universal Lawn Mover from c. 1887. Benthall were later to manufacture motor cars.

What must be the lawn mower enthusiast's dream find is the 1890s steam-powered machine made by the Leyland Motor Company. Various widths of cutters were available from 25 ins to 42 ins, and the weight was from a ½ to 1 ton. The engine was oil-burning and it took ten minutes to raise steam. The operator controlled the machine from the rear and had to tolerate the soot and smoke. Leyland's example was closely followed by steam mowers from Shanks and Greens.

In 1897 Benz of Stuttgart and Coldwell Lawn Mowers of New York both produced petrol-engined mowers, but credit of the first production model must go to Grimsley & Son of Leicester, who marketed motor mowers from 1899.

Ransome entered this field in the early years of the twentieth century and, in 1919, Charles H. Pugh Limited of Birmingham commenced production of what was to become the Atco. In this same year the Derwent Foundry Company Limited of Derby started making a side-wheel machine called the Qualcast.

The Suffolk Iron Foundry was started at Stowmarket by L. J. Tibbenham in 1920 and, in 1925, they produced their first lawn mower.

At an efficiency trial held in Regent's Park by the Royal Horticultural Society in May 1925, ten manufacturers demonstrated twenty-five machines: Thomas Green, Shanks, Atco, Auto-Mower Engineering Company of Bath, Godiva Engineering Company of Slough, Dennis Brothers of Guildford, John Shaw & Sons of Wolverhampton, and F. Mitchell (Nottingham) Limited who made the Atomo.

The MP Company Limited, W. Edgecumbe Readle & Company Limited, and GN Limited (of light car fame), all demonstrated motors to convert hand-propelled mowers.

Ransomes introduced an electric mower in 1926, the first to be driven by this form of power.

For the enthusiast who would like to associate an interest in vintage mowers with motoring history, there are a number of machines to look for. Apart from the Dennis and GN companies already mentioned, there have been those made by the Enfield Cycle Company, Excelsior Motor Company, and JP Super Lawn Mowers of Leicester, the latter being literally the Rolls Royce of mowers—JP was a subsidiary of that venerable car company.

It is hoped that this short history will whet the appetite of potential collectors; it could be extended to cover the revolutionary introduction of such machines as Flymo, but this is a non-specialist book and the author is in danger of being carried away with enthusiasm about one of his favourite subjects. Suffice to say that anyone who wants to be involved with mechanical collecting for little outlay will find mowers rewarding in the extreme.

Further Collecting Suggestions:
Electric Drills and Power Tools
Oil Cans
Record Players
Small Engines (from model aircraft size)

9　Pocket Instruments and Accessories

One of the attractions of collecting personal accessories is that a large number can be conveniently accommodated in a small house without the place looking like a totter's yard. One can go on a buying jaunt without having to carry great loads, and one's partner in marriage is less likely to complain about diminishing family finances than he or she would if a set of Chippendale chairs were delivered or a traction engine was to arrive on a low-loader. Not that either would be bad investments but it is sometimes difficult to convince a less enthusiastic spouse.

Of course, the top end of this collecting division includes snuff boxes, vinaigrettes, pocket watches, fobs and sovereign cases, all now very high and possibly over-priced.

The investing collector would be better advised to aim more down market, going for items in less popular demand, and to wait for fashion to catch up.

Writing Instruments

In a shop in London's Drury Lane, which proudly wears the sign 'His Nibs', is housed the world's largest collection of steel pen nibs: a collection belonging to the stationer, Philip Poole. Many of the nibs are set in their original display cases that the manufacturers' travelling salesmen carried around the country, while others are in the original cardboard boxes with the makers' decorative and colourful labels—names like Perry, Mitchell, Gillott, Hinks Wells & Company, Geo. W. Hughes, Mudie's, Goode & Company, John Heath, and Davy Hammond's 'Crosby' Quills—the labels themselves being fine examples of social ephemera and well deserving to be collected.

Mr Poole believes there are only about a dozen serious collectors of pen nibs which is both surprising and sad: nibs reflect craftsmen's skills and social history—some of them decoratively engraved with motifs such as Napoleon, Queen Victoria, Stephenson's Rocket, and even the Crucifixion scene.

The earliest manufactured steel pen nibs date from the 1820s, the products of several Birmingham factories.

The collecting of pen nibs is strongly recommended. Their size alone makes them suitable for the modern collector with a small house and with family demands on available space.

Although Lewis Edson Waterman is generally attributed with the production of the first fountain pen in 1884, pens containing their own supply of ink are recorded as being sold in Paris as early as 1656. In 1663, Samuel Pepys wrote of being given 'a silver reservoir pen' by William Coventry.

There are a number of examples of self-contained pens in the following century, the first reference to the name 'fountain pen' being in 1710.

In September 1809, a 'compound fountain pen' was patented by that remarkable inventor, Joseph Bramah, who also has to his credit locks, the water closet, and a machine for printing banknotes among his notable engineering achievements. Bramah's pen had a

Fountain pen advertisement, c. 1905.

"SWAN" FOUNTAIN PENS.

NO GIFT CAN APPROACH THEM IN USEFULNESS OR ACCEPTABILITY.

No Dipping. No Shaking. No Scratching. No Blotting.

MADE IN
THREE SIZES,
BUT ONLY
ONE QUALITY—
THE BEST.

Many Points, Patterns, and Mountings.

PRICES—

10/6 TO **£20**

Post free in the U.K.

CATALOGUE POST FREE.

Pens may be posted to all parts of the World.

MABIE, TODD & BARD,
MANUFACTURERS,
93, CHEAPSIDE, LONDON, E.C.
95a, Regent Street, W.; 3, Exchange Street, Manchester; and 37, Ave. de l'Opera, Paris.

SOLD BY ALL STATIONERS.

thin silver tube which was sealed at the end with cork after filling with ink. The silver tube had to be gently squeezed to cause a flow of ink. In 1859 Walter Massey designed and patented the rubber ink sac.

The root of Waterman's invention was in the controlling of the ink flow by allowing air to pass into the ink sac to occupy the space vacated by the ink. Until then no pens had been devised that would deliver the ink to the pen point in a continuous flow, starting and stopping as required by the writer.

In the early 1880s Waterman was selling life insurance in New York City. Competition was plentiful and prospects few. Waterman was prepared to sign up his customers where and when he found them. All applications had to be signed with ink, so he carried with him an ordinary dip pen and a vial of ink. This worked smoothly for some time but there was a constant danger of ink ruining his clothes and important papers and he decided to try out one of the fountain pens of the day. Soon after buying one—we do not know the make—there came a time when a promised large policy had to be signed. With the application completed and only the signature of the prospect to be appended, Waterman tracked him down, tendering the application and fountain pen. Instead of recording the signature, the pen chose to flood ink all over the policy form. Waterman hastened to prepare a duplicate but a rival got there first and the prospect was lost.

Disgusted by the costly behaviour of his fountain pen, Waterman determined to try his latent mechanical talents and devise a really efficient and dependable fountain pen. He realised the problem to be solved was the regulation of the ink flow and, after a study of those already on the market, he decided that a successful application of the principle of capillary attraction would solve his problem. Waterman knew that his feed must not only provide a channel to conduct the ink to the pen nib, but must also permit intake of air to control the ink flow.

Following some failed experiments the idea occurred to cut fissures in the floor of the shallow channel—a fissure alongside each wall—the reasoning being that the fissures would admit the necessary air—thus allowing the ink and air to flow in opposite directions at the same time. It worked but Waterman added a third fissure in the middle of the main channel. It was the fissure feed that was the subject of his U.S. Patent of 12 February 1884.

The original Waterman pen was designed for the use of the

inventor but, as it functioned so well, his friends induced him to give up the insurance business and devote his time to the making of pens. Work was started on a kitchen table at the rear of a cigar shop at the corner of Fulton and Lasseau Streets, New York City, where the output was 200 hand-made pens a year. Each purchaser was given a written personally signed guarantee against any defect.

Fountain pens, at least the twentieth century examples, are reasonably easy to collect, though dealers are becoming increasingly aware of their appeal. Japanese collectors are particularly enthusiastic about writing instruments and several London dealers are reserving any pens that come to hand for this market.

Strange to say, the propelling pencil appeared later than the first fountain pens. In fact it was not until 1863 that it was devised by Johann Faber of Nuremburg. Perhaps the fact that they have often been made in precious metals is the reason that propelling pencils have been collected for some time. It is still a subject with a limited appeal but it can be safely forecast that soon pencils and other writing instruments will be among some of the more sought after items.

Although the propelling pencil is of comparatively recent origin, the pencil, with a graphite rod inserted in a wooden holder can be traced back to 1565, when it was devised by the German scientist Konrad Gresner.

Laslo Biro, hypnotist, sculptor and journalist was editing a cultural magazine in his native Budapest when he devised a ball-point pen in 1938. His aim was to produce a writing instrument that would use a quick-drying ink.

Concerned about the obvious forthcoming domination of Europe by the Nazis, Biro made his way to the Argentine where he continued to work on his invention and was granted a patent on 10 June 1943. In Buenos Aires he happened to meet an Englishman, Henry Martin, who was in South America representing the British Government. Martin saw in the ball-point the answer to a problem that had troubled the Air Ministry through the war— that of leaking ink from pens at high altitudes. He bought the British manufacturing rights and from 1944 started to make leak-proof instruments for the Royal Air Force. His company was called the Miles Martin Pen Company, the Miles part of the concern being that of the aircraft manufacturer who produced the war-time Miles Magister and Master training planes.

With peace in Europe in 1945, the company turned attention to the civilian market, offering Biro pens for £2.15s. (£2.75). A high price then, when the Parker 51 pen could be bought on the Continent for the equivalent of about £4.50. The author recalls buying one of these first civilian Biros in W. H. Smith's at Sevenoaks, Kent, while on leave from Germany around Christmas 1945. It caused considerable interest on returning to Germany but it must be admitted that enthusiasm was inclined to wane when a refill was needed after about a fortnight. The three-folded copper tubes, with a ball set in the tip, could not be readily obtained and were high-priced—about 50 pence if the memory is serving well.

Meanwhile, back in Argentina, the Biro had been sold publicly by the Eterpen Company from early 1945, but Biro had made one very great mistake: he had not patented his invention in the U.S.A., where copies quickly flooded the market.

The early ball-points: Martin-made R.A.F. instruments, the Miles Martin (civilian) Biro, and the Eterpen Biro, are certainly justifiable collectors' items, as are the early throw-away ball-points made in France in the mid-1950s by BIC.

There appears to have been something of a change in public demand since the 1960s, when the throw-away pen was about the only ball-point seen in every-day use. The more expensive refillable ball-points are taking a greater share of the market, and it is time that writing instrument collectors ensured that a representative selection of the throw-away pens is retained. These examples of changes in social habit are in considerable danger of disappearing.

Lighters

Like fountain pens, pocket lighters are much favoured by Japanese collectors and popularity is strengthening in other parts of the world.

Tinder and flint appliances have long had attention from antiquarians but, until recently, the pocket petrol lighter was more than somewhat neglected.

The ancient Greeks and the Romans had flint appliances which could technically be described as lighters. The principle of these early devices was continued well into the sixteenth century. After the introduction of tobacco smoking to England the Elizabethans were finding that it took up to 15 minutes to light a pipe and it would not work at all in a damp or draughty atmosphere. A solution was found in the tinder bag which Elizabethan gentlemen slung on their belts and could be used out-of-doors.

From the seventeenth century to the beginning of the twentieth century, lighters using more advanced means of ignition were developed. Some nineteenth century variations employed paper 'caps' similar to those used in toy pistols, each 'cap' being struck by a hammer or a stylus. Others used more complicated means, such as a vial of acid and metal chips which, together, produced hydrogen gas which was ignited by a spark.

An effective pocket lighter, called The Erie, was manufactured by the Repeating Light Company of Springfield, Mass., under a patent of 7 November 1865.

The introduction of the lighter flint about 1900 marked a considerable advance in lighter design. An Austrian professor, Baron Auer von Welsbach, discovered cerium, the metallic element that forms the basis of the lighter flint. The alloy used by von Welsbach was, logically, known as Auermettall. The first flint igniting lighter was manufactured at the Treibacher factory in Vienna. It had no flint-wheel action, but was a 'strike-lighter', its action being similar to that of a match.

Not until 1909 did the first petrol lighter with a flint-wheel action appear. The name of the flint material, Auermettall, was changed to Mischmetal. The name remains today but the formula has been augmented by the addition of iron and magnesium to improve the quality of sparking.

Ronson (founded in 1919) introduced the first automatic lighter, the Banjo, in 1927. This incorporated a simple thumb-lever action and snuffer which extinguished the flame when released. In 1930, this Ronson design was improved by the introduction of the De-Light. The first 'made in England' Ronson appeared in 1945.

Also in 1945, butane began to be used, a step forward that eventually led to the sealed throw-away lighter, following the expendable ball-point pen and preceding the safety-razor in which the blade is not replaced.

The cheap throw-away lighter presented the publicity people with the chance of producing some interesting promotional gifts and this has added grist to the collectors' mill.

Toothbrushes

The subject may not be to everyone's liking, but collecting

toothbrushes has an appeal to a small hard-core of enthusiasts. They are certainly well-established cosmetic and toilet articles attributed, by some authorities, to the Chinese in the fifteenth century.

There is a recorded reference by Sir Ralph Verney to having a toothbrush sent from Paris in 1649 and, here in Britain, the company of Floris of Jermyn Street, London, have been making them since the eighteenth century.

Nylon was first manufactured in 1938 and the suitability of this material for toothbrushes was quickly realised; Dr West's Miracle Tuft Toothbrush being made in the U.S.A. during that year, before nylon stockings were commercially available.

No toothbrush collection would be anything like complete without an example of an electric toothbrush, preferably one of the first made by the Squibb Company of New York in 1961.

Razors

Safety razor blade labels were collected by a recently deceased publican in Bow, London, who believed he was the pioneer in this field. He probably was, but there is an established and active interest in the collecting of razors themselves; 'cut-throat', safety and electric.

Contrary to popular belief, the idea of a safety razor—one that would not hack pieces of flesh at the slip of an unsteady hand—was not the brainchild of Gillette. As far back as 1771, Jean-Jacques Perret, writer of a book called *Pogonotomy, or the Art of Learning to Shave Oneself*, invented a razor based on a carpenter's plane, with only the edge scraping the skin. In 1828, Sheffield cutlers were selling razors with guards along the edge and this type of shaving device was still common in the early years of the twentieth century.

Hoe-shaped razors, with single-edged blades that could be reground and honed, were being sold in the late 1870s, produced by cutlers of Sheffield and Solingen, Germany. All these were termed 'safety' razors and were meant to reduce the flow of early morning blood.

What King Camp Gillette did was to invent the disposable razor blade, held in a clamp and used once. He had worked on the idea from 1895 and was granted a U.S. Patent in December 1901. Production was begun in 1903 by the American Safety Razor Company of Boston. In that first year only 51 razors and 168 blades were sold. However, by the end of the following year sales had jumped to 90,000 razors and nearly 2½ million blades, and by the time the Gillette razor reached Britain in 1905, the end of the cut-throat razor was in sight.

An interesting letter was recently received from Mr Leonard Bates who has made a point of noting razor history:

> '. . . I joined the army in 1920 and was at the R.A.M.C. Depot at Crookham Camp. That year the Gillette razor supplemented the old "cut-throat" which was general issue. Later the "cut-throat" was withdrawn from the soldier's kit.
>
> I think the Gillette razor was introduced after invitations to tender for the supply of safety razors was put out at that time. Gillette won the contract from the Valet Company, but Valet was not to be completely outwitted and, behold, every soldier in the Depot was presented with a free Valet razor, blades and a strop in a case.'

The first electric razor was manufactured in 1931 by Schick Incorporated of Stamford, Connecticut. Since then they have been made the world over in all shapes and sizes.

Electricity is the most popular power for mechanical shaving but there have been other sources. Clockwork and inertia motors have been used in production models; one inertia motor powered razor being of the Viceroy range made by the Rolls Razor Company. Frankly, it was rather a useless instrument that depended on a contracting and expanding grip of the fingers to keep the motor going, thus making it extremely difficult to hold during the shaving operation. Needless to say, this razor was not in production for long and is, in consequence, something of a rarity.

A collection of powered razors may not be the last word in aesthetic appeal but they are undeniably interesting and certainly hold a potential as future collectables.

10   Toys and Models

Men are always boys at heart. A sweeping statement perhaps, but one with more than an element of truth, as can be witnessed by the average age of those attending model exhibitions. The same may well be true of women but they are inclined to be less demonstrative, if only in this respect! However, it is true to say that collectors of dolls, dolls' houses, dolls' house furniture, and soft toys are largely female. And a very strong corps it is too.

In 1960, after 28 years of collecting die-cast model cars, the first—a Tootsietoy Graham Paige Blue Streak—being bought on a visit to Woolworth's at the age of six, the writer felt it was about time to confirm, one way or another, if his mental age was retarded. A letter for publication was sent to a prominent motoring journal, asking if such a collecting activity was unusual for one of advanced years. The feedback of over 150 letters from others of around the same age who generally admitted to similar doubts as to their maturity, was reassuring, and we now know that there are many thousand die-cast model car collectors throughout the world who are willing to pay high prices for out-of-production models. Some have been known to treble their value immediately following the end of the production run.

The moral of this little story is that no one need feel ashamed of their collecting interests—there are many more fellow 'nutters' around than we are inclined to think—regardless of what friends and relatives tell us.

Soft Toys

There is something about the dear old Teddy Bear that appeals to people of all ages. Books have been written about him and he has had some decent television and radio coverage, mainly through the enthusiastic efforts of actor Peter Bull, probably the best known collector of this specific toy. It may be becoming too late to get in on the ground floor of Teddy Bear collecting, but it is still just possible to buy venerable examples at reasonable prices.

The 18 November 1902 issue of the *Washington Evening Star* featured a Clifford Berryman cartoon showing President Theodore 'Teddy' Roosevelt refusing to shoot a captive bear cub. It is said that this was founded on an actual incident.

Probably the first Teddy Bears were made by a Brooklyn sweetshop owner, Morris Mitchom, who produced a short handmade run. This claim is disputed by some authorities who state that the Teddy Bear originated in Germany in that year, 1902.

Germany was certainly the home of soft toys from 1880 when Margaret Steiff of Giengen produced felt elephants, probably the first soft toys to be made.

On the other hand, blackfaced rag dolls were sold at American country fairs in the mid-nineteenth century and it was on dolls such as these that Florence K. Upton based the 'golliwog' character for her book, *The Adventures of Two Dutch Dolls and a Golliwog*, published in 1895.

Florence Upton's original golliwog was auctioned at Christies' in 1917, when it reached 450 guineas, to raise money for the Red Cross. The purchaser presented the golliwog to the Prime Minister and it has since remained at Chequers, the premier's country residence.

Like other playthings, soft toys, both old and new, are sound investments, particularly if they have a known history or if made by a famous toy maker and kept in pristine condition.

Lead and Die-Cast Toys

It is a few years too late to suggest lead toys as a subject to collect for investment. Almost anything of lead, whether it be military, circus, farmyard or zoo, has reached astronomical prices and it would seem unlikely that this will proportionately rise in the next few years to make investment worthwhile.

A better proposition is that of new die-cast model (toy) cars, some of which, if carefully selected, can be worth twice the original retail price within about a year of purchase. One such model was a Corgi Bentley that appeared a few years back in their catalogue marked 'out of production' even before it was stocked in the shops. The makers were at that time undergoing a policy change about the wheels fitted to their models.

Like lead toys, die-cast models of a few years back are extremely

Television 'spin-off' models come in all sizes: this—from the *Thunderbirds* series—is 22ft long.

A novelty car of more collectable proportions.

STRIPEY - the Magic Mini 107

highly priced and, again, like their lead counterparts, would seem to be an unattractive investment unless bought cheaply at jumble sales. Picking new model investment prospects, like that of the Corgi Bentley, is not easy. Another way that some people play the market is to watch the new catalogues and, when a model is not included, to go round the shops buying as many mint and boxed examples as possible.

Die-cast models of vehicles featured in films and television series can be a reasonable investment. An example of this kind of model is the James Bond 'Goldfinger' Aston Martin, of which Corgi produced two versions—one winning a Toy of the Year award. It is the smaller of these two versions that collectors prefer.

Tinplate Toys

It has long been realised that the tinplate toys of the Victorian era, and those made up to the outbreak of World War II, are highly desirable and collectable. However, it is not so generally appreciated that tinplate toys have, over the past very few years, virtually disappeared from the world's toy shops; the ease and cheapness of manufacture of plastic toys, together with a complex tangle of regulations concerning the safety of toys, have caused them to be not only a dirty word in the toy trade, but material to be considered by collectors for tomorrow.

Tinplate toys are some of the easiest things to collect without specialist knowledge as, in common with almost anything bought new and kept in pristine condition, they are certain to gain value with the passing years. Those interested in knowing more about the subject are recommended to read Michael Buhler's book, *Tin Toy 1945–1975* (Bergstrom & Boyle, 1978).

Flying Models and Toys

Because of their frailty, flying model aircraft are not good survivors. Consequently, they possess that quality dearly loved by collectors; that of rarity.

It is a remarkable fact that flying model aircraft have a far longer history than their full-sized counterparts, which gives them a mystique unique in the field of working models, going back to 1848, when the first powered flight was made by a steam-driven

An early model flying machine.

Assembled cardboard cut-outs.

twin-screw model monoplane by John Stringfellow at Chard, Somerset.

Rubber-band powered flight was first achieved in Paris in 1871, when Alphonse Penard's *Phlanaphore* flew a distance of 131 feet. This type of power for models is still in use today.

Sometimes one can find some pre-World War II FROG models made by International Model Aircraft. These are real treasures for the enthusiast. As a boy, the author looked longingly in toyshop windows at the beautiful FROG Hawker Hind, but the £2 price was far more than could be afforded. The Hawker Hind is still being sought!

Meccano

Meccano is one of the outstanding twentieth century success stories in the constructional toy field. Born in 1863, Frank Hornby, son of a Liverpool provision merchant, had an intense interest in engineering and mechanics. Despite this he worked for a company of Liverpool meat importers until he was 45 years of age.

It was his love of making toys for his children that led him to invent the model constructional system that was to become known the world over as Meccano. The first patent was taken out on 9 January 1901, claiming that this was the basic principles of engineering applied to a metal constructional toy.

Originally marketed as 'Mechanics Made Easy', the system was not called Meccano until 1907, the name being registered on 14 September of that year.

The story of part number 54, 'Perforated Flanged Sector Plate', is typical of most of the individual Meccano parts. Although it is not mentioned as a numbered part in a catalogue until 1911, many authoritative collectors think the first version of flanged sector plate was introduced *c.* 1906. The original version was 4 ins long and had a single row of three holes crossed by a top row of five and a lower row of three holes.

When this was changed to the second pattern is not certain, but as far as the United Kingdom is concerned, it was probably in 1911. It was the same shape and size as the first version but had three rows of eight holes. By this time the parts were being made in America by the Meccano factory there, and the perforated plate was the subject of U.S. Patent 1079245 (Application date 14

Meccano construction.

A gem for tinplate toy collectors: a wind-up pulley waggon made by a
German manufacturer in 1904.

October 1912. Granted 18 November 1913). Parts were not separately patented in the U.K.

What is not known is whether the first pattern, with the single row of eight holes, was made in the U.S.A.

The U.S. Meccano factory was taken over in 1928 by A. C. Gilbert (of model railroad fame) and the parts were made at Newhaven, Conn., under the name 'Erector'. Their manual shows part 54 as the same as the second type Liverpool pattern.

The third pattern, $4\frac{1}{2}$ ins long, with three rows of nine holes, was introduced by the Liverpool factory in December 1934 as part 54A, reverting to the old 54 number in 1940, by which time stocks of the old pattern had run out.

The really valuable Meccano parts are those in the assembly designated in the catalogues as 167, Geared Roller Bearing, made between 1928 and 1940. This is rare enough to fetch in excess of £40 when complete (1977 figure).

The following, though not intended to be regarded as 100 per cent. reliable, is a useful guide when dating Meccano parts:

Until 1924, parts were nickel-plated;
From 1924 until early 1939, parts were painted red and green;
In 1939 a blue and gold combination of colours was adopted by the Liverpool factory, following an earlier example of the associated company in France. The Liverpool factory also made matt green and black parts with fewer holes for military construction sets.
From 1964 a yellow and blue colour combination has been used.

Meccano clubs are active in many parts of Britain and a large percentage of their membership is by no means young. The author recently spent an intriguing Saturday afternoon at a meeting of the Holy Trinity Meccano Club at Hildenborough, Kent—a club that was first affiliated to the Meccano Guild in the early 1920s. The exhibits at that meeting included replicas of Brunel's Portsmouth Block Making Machinery and an extraordinary exercise called the Chinese Chariot on which an arm pointed to the south no matter the direction or the speed at which the chariot was moved. The exercise was to make one of these chariots with the smallest number of gears. The winner, who was something of an inventive mechanical genius, built his chariot with only two gears.

There must be thousands of vintage Meccano parts dormant in attics and now would seem to be the time to bring them out.

123

For one who believes that there should be more to collecting than simply buying one or two expensive and beautiful craftsman-made pieces, it is hard to understand the trend in recent years of producing de luxe chess and backgammon sets. Sometimes one sees nine-men's-morris games of similar standard and it is perhaps significant that these are the games that are commonly thought to demand skills of superior intellect. It is also noteworthy that we do not see de luxe ludo or snakes and ladders boards, leather covered and tooled in gold.

It could be argued that an extensive collection of packs of children's card games is of greater social interest than the chess and backgammon and it is conceivable that, whereas the craftsman-made product may gain 50 per cent. in value over five years, the mass-produced card games *en masse* may appreciate a great deal more if the collection includes printing variations and out of production games. It is an old and proven maxim of speculative investment that the scope of the portfolio should be wide and eggs should not be put in one basket.

Darts

Time was, a very few years ago, when an after work game of darts in a pub was a modest and inexpensive pastime. It was a 'cloth cap' game and equipment was simple. In the late 1950s and '60s interest waned and it was not until the television programmers saw that it could make good viewing that the game of darts had a revival.

The opportunity was quickly grasped by the marketing boys who, blinding people with 'technology', pursuaded players that it was impossible to play well without slim tungsten-pointed precision-turned darts, sets of which can cost as much as a second-hand car. Observation of games in progress does not indicate any improvement in accuracy or consistency of aim over the past two decades, but surely nobody would pay up to £50 for a set of darts just for a piece of 'one-upmanship'—or would they?

This sophistication has led the wide-scale rejection of the old style of darts and before long it will be hard to find any of the simple hand-arrows, which must mean they will become collectors' items and that they will gain some value as such.

In a charming little book, published in 1936, called *Darts*, Rupert Croft-Cooke describes the darts of the period:

'There is the heavy brass dart, with paper or celluloid flight—a popular weapon in the home counties. It is probably more accurate than the feather dart, but it has certain disadvantages. Its very weight and shape often robs its flight of directness, and it crashes flat against the board instead of piercing it and scoring. It is the dart of lorry-drivers, road-workers, and those fine performers— brewers' draymen. It goes home happily enough, but it causes delays by losing its flights or requiring new ones at a critical moment.

'The feather dart is a more delicate thing. It is made in all sizes, and obtainable weighted and unweighted. The unweighted type, a mere smooth pencil of wood with a metal point and goose feather flight to it, is not for the amateurs, but a deadly accurate weapon in the hand of an artist . . . It needs very neat and steady handling, it must be thrown with precisely uniform force, but to see it in the hands of a really fine player is a joy.

'The commonest, and for the normal player the most commendable dart is the weighted feather one. It combines the grim accuracy of the brass with the sagittal flight of the unweighted feather. It is also the type most commonly provided for general use by publicans, so that to be accustomed to it saves a good deal of trouble. It has the additional advantage of wearing well, for when there is no weight on a dart its feathers must be in perfect trim, but on a weighted dart the fact that they are a little worn or twisted (moulting to use the general term), will not completely ruin the game.'

That dated description, very much of the 1930s, is a good survey of the darts used in the period. Not many have survived from that time, though the author recently acquired some feather darts that had been bricked up in a pub cupboard since 1933—a veritable time capsule with advertisements and showcards of the period.

The time is surely right to start a museum of pub games, preferably in their natural environment. Enterprising brewers please note.

Further Collecting Suggestions:

Building Bricks: the first of which were marketed by Minton in 1843 under the name, Henry Cole's *Box of Terra Cotta Bricks*.

Craze Toys: one of the greatest was the Yo-Yo marketed by Louis Marx of New York from 1929.

Cut Outs: started with paper dolls on sale in London from 1791.

Plastic Kits (unmade)
Betting Slips and Bookmakers' Material
Card and Board Games
Dice and Dice Shakers
Gambling Machine Tokens
Sporting Programmes
Sports Headgear

11   Time Capsule Collecting

Under Cleopatra's Needle, erected on Victoria Embankment in 1878, there lies a casket containing outfits of men's and women's clothes of the period, coins and newspapers; an early example of the now extensive practice of embodying time capsules in the foundations of new buildings and statuary.

Time capsules, in one form or another, are commonly in the hands of people who would never claim to be collectors. A bundle of love letters, a shoe box of wedding photographs and relics, or souvenirs of a memorable holiday.

This is one area outside the many themes already suggested in this book. Generally the objects in a personal or family time capsule have little or no intrinsic value and the collection is assembled with no view to profit: they are there as memory makers, to be brought out and enjoyed from time to time.

Profit aside, one need not treat the opening of the personal time capsule solely as the opportunity for self-indulgent nostalgia or for humming 'These Foolish Things' or 'Among My Souvenirs'. The time capsule collection can be of genuine social significance.

Eminently convenient items are public transport tickets. Surely someone, somewhere, in 1837, put away one of the first cardboard dated and numbered railway tickets that were devised and issued by Thomas Edmondson, a booking clerk at Mitton Station on the Newcastle and Carlisle Railway. Perhaps someone else, in 1880, thought it would be a good idea to save a set of the very first bus tickets, all three: 1d, 2d and 3d, which were introduced by the London and District Bus Company. Lowest available fare bus tickets are always useful ingredients for a time capsule, particularly in these days of ever rising prices.

A nice small piece of social history would have been a 1950 Diners' Club card issued in the United States; the first of a mushroom field of credit cards.

Photographs and picture postcards are always popular time capsule items. The most valuable—from the historical if not mercenary angle—are those showing street scenes and costume. As mentioned earlier in this book, there is no greater scene of change than the High Street, and no more subtle, almost undetectable, transformation than that of attire under the steady influence of commercial fashion. Snapshots of family groups in the garden may bring back memories, but if we must take a photo of visiting Aunt Jane, let's try and do it in the street with a few vehicles, lamp standards and road signs in the background.

By a roundabout on the A21, just outside the Greater London boundary, lives a gentleman with an unusual hobby. Since the early 1930s, when roundabouts first appeared, he has photographed all the street furniture—Keep Left signs etc.—that have been at this roundabout and on a mile stretch of the road. Because of the number of times careless drivers have knocked down the signs, his collection numbers several hundred. They have proved invaluable to local and transport historians and for settling arguments in the local press.

For the majority of people who want to put together personal time capsules, space is of primary importance. Whatnots, so adored by Victorians and used up to World War II for the display of crested china, were ideal for small attractive displays, using one shelf for each commemoration. Plain, modern bookshelves may be used in the same way.

Not all time capsule relics are suitable for 'open' display. Printed pieces, ephemera, fades in living room conditions, and tickets, billheads and programmes laying around on shelves make the place look as if tidying-up chores have been neglected. Most addicts resort to the Old Faithful cardboard box and many an ancient dog-eared shoe box has done sterling service in this rôle. Metal boxes are better, biscuit tins (themselves highly collectable) and filing boxes that can be bought from office stationers—they also sell plastic containers that serve the purpose. Apart from durability, the advantage of a metal or plastic capsule is that it can be made airtight by the stick-on foam strip used on doors for excluding draughts.

The simplest social history time capsule to put down annually like a pipe of port would be a set of nation-wide Yellow Page Directories, a Green Shield Trading Stamp catalogue to show trends in 'good life' homes, and a few issues of Weekend colour magazines to point the way that popular culture is going, or has gone!